W9-CGN-573

ANTITRUST ECONOMICS ON TRIAL

*A Dialogue on the
New Laissez-Faire*

ANTITRUST ECONOMICS ON TRIAL

A Dialogue on the New Laissez-Faire

WALTER ADAMS AND
JAMES W. BROCK

PRINCETON UNIVERSITY PRESS

Library of Congress Cataloging-in-Publication Data

Adams, Walter, 1922 Aug. 27–
Antitrust economics on trial : a dialogue on the new laissez-faire /
Walter Adams and James W. Brock.
p. cm.
Includes index.
ISBN 0-691-04291-8 — ISBN 0-691-00391-2 (pbk.)
1. Trusts, Industrial—United States. 2. Consolidation
and merger of corporations—United States. 3. Trade
regulation—United States. 4. Antitrust law—United States.
5. Competition—Government policy—United States.
I. Brock, James W. II. Title.
HD2795.A23   1991
338.8—dc20   91-17176

This book has been composed in Linotron Trump

10 9 8 7 6 5 4 3 2 1
10 9 8 7 6 5 4 3 2 1
(Pbk.)

FOR

Frank Hyneman Knight
(1885–1972)

IN MEMORIAM

CONTENTS

LIST OF EXHIBITS

FOR SOME twenty-five years, a shrill cacophony of divergent opinion has marked the debate on U.S. antitrust policy. Theorists against empiricists. Apostles of the Chicago-based New Learning against defenders of the traditional structure/conduct/performance paradigm. "Laissez-faire" advocates against "interventionists." "Neoconservatives" against "neoliberals."

Aside from the arguments of those who believe that antitrust is a counterproductive anachronism and should be abolished altogether, the debate has centered on the proper role of antitrust in a free enterprise economy. Is the central purpose of antitrust to promote a decentralized decisionmaking mechanism, or is it simply to promote a maximum of "consumer welfare"? Does concentration of power in the hands of a single firm or a few firms matter, or can we rely on the market to erode monopoly and oligopoly power? How should economic power be measured in the relevant product market and geographic market? Is there a trade-off between market dominance and superior efficiency? If so, how can it be measured, and how should the divergence be resolved? In this context, what is an appropriate policy toward mergers generally, and toward horizontal, vertical, and conglomerate mergers specifically? What scientific and practical guidelines are at hand to formulate a rational and workable policy on mergers?

Aficionados of the theater of the absurd[1] would find the character of the debate intimately familiar. There is an absence of communication—a terrifying diversity of utterances, with the actors on stage listening only to snatches and fragments of the dialogue, and responding as if they had not listened at all. At times the dialogue consists of statements that are in and of themselves perfectly lucid and logically constructed but lacking in context and relevance. At other times, absurd ideas are proclaimed as if they were eternal truths. In this dialogue of the deaf, the actors are animated by the certitude and unshakable nature of their basic assumptions—one side relying on the wisdom of past experience, the other prepared to sweep away the beliefs that have been tested and found wanting, beliefs they consider illusions and self-deceptions.

Above all, there is a degradation of language—a recourse to verbal banality. In an age of mass communication, language has run riot. Words border on the meaningless and lack authentic content. Often, dialogue consists of little more than ossified clichés, empty formulas, and popular slogans—a vulgarization of ideology.

Why did we write this book? Why this choice of genre to address a professional audience? Primarily to put in perspective the polemical books and pre-

---

[1] See Martin Esslin, *The Theater of the Absurd* (New York: Anchor Books, 1961). For specimens of the genre, see plays by Samuel Becket, Arthur Adamov, Eugene Ionesco, and Vaclav Havel. For a pioneering venture by an economist as playwright, see Leonard Silk, *Veblen: A Play in Three Acts* (New York: A. M. Kelley Publishers, 1966).

tentiously "scientific" articles that have done little to resolve the public policy debate. Primarily to lay bare the states of mind and images that constitute the hidden assumptions in the debate—to provide an intersection between what is visible and what is under the surface, to expose the latent content that forms the essence of the controversy. Primarily to expose the disguised meaning of the words used by the protagonists in the debate. Our dialogue finds absurdity not in the depths of the irrational, but in what on the surface appears to be rational. It seeks to demonstrate that "a false vocabulary systematically places the debate on false ground and makes it practically impossible to analyze the concrete reality."[2]

The setting is a voir dire[3] in a U.S. district court hearing a merger case. An exponent of the New Laissez-Faire is being examined to determine whether he/she is qualified to provide testimony as an economic expert. The expert is not set up as a straw man uttering lines concocted by partisan playwrights. His/her words are amply documented and accurately reflect the worldview of the so-called New Learning (Chicago school), which is currently popular in the federal judiciary. Our purpose is not

[2] Milan Kundera, "Candide Had to Be Destroyed," in Jan Vladislav, ed., *Vaclav Havel, or Living in Truth* (London: Faber and Faber, 1986), 261.

[3] A voir dire (literally, "to speak the truth") is a judicial proceeding in which a witness is examined to determine his or her qualifications and competence to testify as an expert. See *Black's Law Dictionary*, 5th ed. (1979), 1412.

to preach a sermon or to impart a message or to declare a winner. That is a task for the reader.

In Ionesco's *The Bald Soprano*, Mrs. Martin asks "What is the message?" The Fireman replies, "That is for you to find out."

ANTITRUST
ECONOMICS ON
TRIAL

*A Dialogue on the
New Laissez-Faire*

*The dialogue takes place
in a courtroom.
The participants are
a judge, an attorney,
and an expert witness.*

Day 1 – The Trial Begins; The Witness Defines Price Theory

JUDGE: We shall now proceed with the voir dire requested by the Government.

ATTORNEY: Thank you, Your Honor. [*To the witness*] Please state for the record your current occupation and title.

EXPERT: I am currently professor of economics at the University of Chicago, a fellow at the Cato Institute, and a consultant to the Heritage Foundation.

ATTORNEY: The Cato Institute and the Heritage Foundation are self-styled libertarian think tanks?

EXPERT: They are research organizations inspired by the laissez-faire philosophy and dedicated to the preservation of free enterprise institutions.

ATTORNEY: What other professional experience have you had?

EXPERT: After receiving my doctorate from the University of Chicago, I served as an assistant professor of economics at the University of Rochester and an associate professor at UCLA. During my sabbatical year, I was chief economist in the Justice Department's antitrust division; at the time, Professor William Baxter of the Stanford Law School was assistant attorney general in charge of the division. In addition

I have served as an economic consultant to the governments of Chile and Poland.

ATTORNEY: I assume you have published widely in your field?

EXPERT: Yes. I have published numerous books and articles on such topics as game theory, Cournot duopoly, contestability, dynamic Nash equilibria, optimal two-part tariffs, opportunism and self-disbelieved behavior, as well as public choice models of antitrust and other forms of government intervention. My articles have appeared in the *Journal of Economic Theory*, the *Journal of Political Economy*, the *Journal of Law and Economics*, the *Journal of Business*, and the *University of Chicago Law Review*.

ATTORNEY: With the exception of the *Journal of Economic Theory*, would I be correct in assuming that the other journals you mentioned are all published by the University of Chicago?

EXPERT: That is correct.

ATTORNEY: Would you tell us, Professor, what you consider to be your special field of expertise.

The Testimony on the Scope of Price Theory

EXPERT: Price theory.

ATTORNEY: Could you define that, please?

EXPERT: It is the science explaining rational economic behavior and the operation of markets.

ATTORNEY: And what is its relevance to law?

EXPERT: Its relevance is much broader.

ATTORNEY: What do you mean?

EXPERT: In recent years, economists have used price theory more boldly in an effort to explain behavior beyond the narrow confines of the business world, and many noneconomists have followed their example. We have developed economic theories to explain racial discrimination,[4] human fertility,[5] crime,[6] marriage and the family,[7] divorce,[8] suicide,[9] drug ad-

[4] Gary S. Becker, *The Economics of Discrimination*, 2d ed. (Chicago: University of Chicago Press, 1971).

[5] Gary S. Becker, "An Economic Analysis of Fertility," in National Bureau of Economic Research Conference, *Demographic and Economic Change in Developed Countries* (Princeton, N.J.: Princeton University Press, 1960); Willis, "A New Approach to the Economic Theory of Fertility," *Journal of Political Economy* 81 (1973).

[6] See sources cited in notes 13–15.

[7] Gary S. Becker, *A Treatise on the Family* (Cambridge: Harvard University Press, 1981); id., "A Theory of Marriage," Parts 1, 2 *Journal of Political Economy* 81, 82 (1973, 1974); T. W. Schultz, ed., *Economics of the Family: Marriage, Children, and Human Capital* (1975); G. S. Becker and H. G. Lewis, "On the Interaction between the Quantity and Quality of Children," *Journal of Political Economy* 81 (1973); D. DeTray, "Child Quality and the Demand for Children," *Journal of Political Economy* 81 (1973); A. Freiden, "The United States Marriage Market," *Journal of Political Economy* 82 (1974); R. T. Michael, "Education and the Derived Demand for Children," *Journal of Political Economy* 81 (1973).

[8] Gary S. Becker, Elisabeth M. Landes, and Robert T. Michael, "An Economic Analysis of Marital Instability," *Journal of Political Economy* 85 (1977): 1141. Applying price theory, the authors demonstrate that "women who become pregnant accidentally while searching for a mate have an incentive to marry quickly, even if they have not completed their search, because of their desire to 'legitimate' their children, and because they become less valuable to other potential mates. Put differently, they are more likely to accept a mismatch because the cost to them of additional intensive and extensive search has increased. Therefore, accidental premarital conceptions should increase the probability of marital dissolution" (p. 1151).

[9] Daniel S. Hamermesh and Neal M. Sos, "An Economic Theory of Suicide," *Journal of Political Economy* 82 (Jan./Feb. 1974).

diction,[10] politics,[11] education,[12] etc.[13] Indeed, economic theory is singularly useful in providing a unified framework for understanding *all* behavior involving scarce resources, both market and nonmarket, both monetary and nonmonetary.[14]
ATTORNEY: Could you give us some examples?
EXPERT: Take crime, for example. As Professor Gary Becker argued in a seminal article,[15] criminals are

[10] See Gary S. Becker, Michael Grossman, and Kevin M. Murphy, "Rational Addiction and the Effect of Price on Consumption," Working Paper no. 68, Center for the Study of the Economy and the State, University of Chicago (Feb. 1991).

[11] Gary S. Becker, "Competition and Democracy," *Journal of Law and Economics* 1 (1958): 105–9; Downs, "An Economic Theory of Political Action in a Democracy," *Journal of Political Economy* 67 (1957).

[12] Gary S. Becker, *Human Capital: A Theoretical and Empirical Analysis* (New York: Columbia University Press, 1964, 1975); Sam Peltzman, "The Effect of Government Subsidies-in-Kind on Private Expenditures: The Case of Higher Education," *Journal of Political Economy* 81 (1973); T. W. Schultz, "The Formation of Human Capital by Education," *Journal of Political Economy* 68 (1960).

[13] For a somewhat strained application of price theory, see Jeff E. Biddle and Daniel S. Hamermesh, "Sleep and the Allocation of Time," National Bureau of Economic Research Working Paper no. 2988 (May 1989). For a delightfully amusing application of price theory to the solution of murder mysteries, see Marshall Jevons [William Breit and Kenneth Elzinga], *Murder at the Margin* (Sun Lakes, Ariz.: Thos. Horton & Daughters, 1978); and id., *The Fatal Equilibrium* (Cambridge: MIT Press, 1985).

[14] Gary S. Becker, *The Economic Approach to Human Behavior* (Chicago: University of Chicago Press, 1976), 205.

[15] Gary S. Becker, "Crime and Punishment: An Economic Approach," *Journal of Political Economy* 76 (1968): 169–217. See also Gary S. Becker and William Landes, eds., *Essays in the Economics of Crime and Punishment* (National Bureau of Economic Research, 1974); Simon Rottenberg, ed., *The Economics of Crime and Punishment* (Washington, D.C.: American Enterprise Institute, 1973); Isaac Ehrlich, "Participation in Illegitimate Activities: A Theoretical and Empirical Investigation," *Journal of Political Economy* 81 (1973); id., "Capital Punishment: A Case of Life or Death," *American Economic Review* (June 1975). For an empirical/econometric analysis, see Peter Schmidt and Ann D. Witte, *An Economic Analysis of Crime and Justice* (Orlando, Fla.: Academic Press, 1984).

about like anyone else. They rationally maximize their own self-interest (utility), subject to the constraints (prices, incomes) that they face in the marketplace and elsewhere. Thus the decision to become a criminal is in principle no different from the decision to become a bricklayer or a carpenter, or, indeed, an economist.[16]

ATTORNEY: It is all a very rational process?

EXPERT: That is correct. Price theory demonstrates that punishment will deter crime.

ATTORNEY: Could you explain?

EXPERT: The reason is perfectly simple: Demand curves slope downward. If you increase the cost of an article, less of it will be consumed. Similarly, if you increase the cost of committing a crime, fewer crimes will be committed. The elasticity of the demand curve, of course, has to be taken into consideration. If the elasticity is low, the quantitative effect of raising the cost of engaging in delinquency will be relatively small. If the elasticity is high, the effect will be great.[17]

ATTORNEY: Can you furnish some other examples?

---

[16] Paul H. Rubin, "The Economics of Crime," *Atlantic Economic Review* 28 (1978): 38. Similarly, Professor (now Judge) Richard Posner views the criminal as "someone who has chosen to engage in criminal activity because the expected utility of such activity to him, net of expected costs, is greater than that of any legitimate alternative activity." Richard Posner, *Economic Analysis of Law* (Boston: Little, Brown & Co., 1973), 365.

[17] Gordon Tullock, "Does Punishment Deter Crime?" *The Public Interest* (Summer 1974), reprinted in Ralph Andreano and John J. Siegfried, eds., *The Economics of Crime* (Cambridge, Mass.: Schenkman Publishing Co., 1980), 127–36, 129. See also Gordon Tullock, "An Economic Approach to Crime," *Social Science Quarterly* 50 (1969): 59–71.

EXPERT: Like other human behavior, marriage and divorce can be explained in terms of price theory:[18] A person decides to marry when the utility expected from marriage exceeds that expected from remaining single or from additional search for a more suitable mate.[19] Similarly, a married person terminates his or her marriage when the utility anticipated from becoming single or marrying someone else exceeds the loss in utility from separation, including losses due to physical separation from one's children, division of joint assets, legal fees, and so forth. Since many persons are looking for mates, there is a marriage *market*: Each person tries to do the best he or she can, given that everyone else in the market is trying to do the best they can. A sorting of persons into different marriages is said to be in equilibrium if persons not married to each other in this sorting could not marry and make each better off.[20]

ATTORNEY: It's all a matter of simple, rational calculation?

EXPERT: Yes. For example, the physical and emotional involvement called love has an important economic component. The calculation may be conscious or un-

[18] Becker, *Economic Approach to Human Behavior*. Says Becker: "Two simple principles form the heart of the analysis. The first is that, since marriage is practically always voluntary, either by the persons marrying or their parents, the theory of preferences can be readily applied, and persons marrying (or their parents) can be assumed to expect to raise their utility level above what it would be were they to remain single. The second is that, since many men and women compete as they seek mates, a *market* in marriages can be presumed to exist" (p. 206).

[19] Ibid., ch. 11.

[20] Ibid.

conscious, explicit or implicit, but it has to be made in order to arrive at a utility-maximizing decision.

ATTORNEY: What does that mean?

EXPERT: By sharing the same household, persons in love can reduce the cost of frequent contact and of resource transfers between each other.[21]

ATTORNEY: Any other examples?

EXPERT: Yes, take decisions with respect to family size, for instance. Children are much like cars, houses, and machinery. They can be considered consumer durables, which provide utility to their parents. Via a utility function or a set of indifference curves, the utility from children can be compared with that derived from other goods. The net cost of children can easily be computed.[22]

ATTORNEY: How do you make such a computation?

EXPERT: In principle, the net cost of children equals the present value of expected outlays plus the imputed value of the parents' services, minus the present value of the expected money return plus the imputed value of the child's services. If net costs are positive, children constitute a consumer durable yielding psychic income or utility. If net costs are negative, children would constitute a producer good yielding pecuniary income. The family can select children of many different qualities—its selection being determined by family tastes, family income, and each child's price. Most families in recent years have made very large net expenditures on children.[23]

[21] Ibid., 210.
[22] Ibid., 173.
[23] Ibid., 175.

ATTORNEY: Are you saying that decisions on family size are determined by strictly economic decisions?

EXPERT: By no means. Sociological considerations—factors such as race, religion, and cultural heritage—are subsumed in the "tastes" category in our formula. They are part of the framework. The point is that by using economic theory we are able to analyze fertility trends scientifically.[24]

ATTORNEY: Do you have other such esoteric examples of how economic theory explains human behavior?

EXPERT: You may find these examples esoteric—and even amusing—but they do demonstrate the explanatory power and ubiquitous relevance of economic theory. Take extramarital affairs. Price theorists have developed a model that explains how a married person allocates his or her time among work, spouse, and paramour. The philanderer sees the value (or cost) of time spent with the paramour as a function of his/her own wage rate and nonlabor income, the time spent by the spouse in the marriage, the value of goods supplied by the spouse to the marriage, the time spent by the paramour in the affair, the value of goods supplied by the paramour to the affair, etc. These are the kinds of considerations that impact on the utility received from the marriage and the utility received from the affair.[25]

[24] Ibid., 173.
[25] Ray C. Fair, "A Theory of Extramarital Affairs," Cowles Foundation Paper no. 457 (New Haven: Cowles Foundation for Research in Economics, 1978), 46.

ATTORNEY: Let me see if I understand you correctly. Does the rational choice model,[26] which you have articulated and which you believe applies to the most diverse types of human behavior, imply that individual economic decisionmakers never make mistakes?

EXPERT: Stated more accurately, the model implies that if, ex post, a decision appears to have been mistaken, either at the individual level (in the sense of having failed to maximize expected utility or profit or some other maximand) or at the social level (in the sense of being Pareto inefficient), either type of mistake is attributable to well-known market imperfections. In the case of individual mistakes, the conventional explanation is that the decisionmaker lacked the appropriate information and that had he or she had that information, he or she would have behaved differently, in a clearly utility-maximizing way.[27]

ATTORNEY: Is there not an alternative explanation for errors in decisionmaking? Does not recent work in cognitive psychology provide a mounting body of evidence suggesting that the rational choice model routinely used by economists—including the subjective expected utility model of decisionmaking under uncertainty—is not complete and therefore may neither accurately describe nor predict actual decisionmaking?

EXPERT: Could you clarify that question?

---

[26] For a discussion of this model, see Robert D. Cooter and Thomas S. Ulen, *Law and Economics* (Glenview, Ill.: Scott, Foresman, 1988).

[27] Thomas S. Ulen, "Criticisms of the Theory of Rational Choice and Their Implications for the Economic Analysis of Legal Rules" (Paper presented at Michigan State University, Nov. 11, 1990), 2–3.

ATTORNEY: The thrust of this evidence seems to indicate that many, perhaps most, individuals routinely make errors in the processing of routine information. The implication of this finding is that individuals may make many more errors in their attempts to maximize their utility or profit than the rational choice model assumes. Actions like smoking a cigarette, having a drink, or eating a candy bar all lead to immediate and certain gratification, whereas their bad consequences are remote in time, only probabilistic, and still avoidable now. It is no contest: certain and immediate rewards win out over probabilistic and remote costs, even though the rewards are slight and the possible costs lethal.[28]

EXPERT: Unlike economics, cognitive psychology is not an exact science. The conclusions you have advanced are entirely hypothetical and speculative.

ATTORNEY: Isn't it true that not only psychologists but some very distinguished economists would raise questions about your rational choice model and its applications? For example, hasn't Professor James Buchanan, a Nobel laureate—and, incidentally, your classmate at Chicago—pointed out that "the theory of choice presents a paradox. If the utility function of the choosing agent is fully defined in advance, choice becomes purely mechanical. No 'decision,' as such is required; there is no weighing of alternatives. On the other hand, if the utility function is not

---

[28] See George A. Akerlof, "Procrastination and Obedience," *AEA Papers and Proceedings* 81 (May 1991):5; Robyn Dawes, *Rational Choice in an Uncertain World* (San Diego: Harcourt Brace Jovanovich, 1988); and Detlef von Winterfeldt and Ward Edwards, *Decision Analysis and Behavioral Research* (New York: Cambridge University Press, 1986).

wholly defined, choice becomes real, and decisions
become unpredictable mental events. If I know what
I want, a computer can make all of my choices for
me. If I do not know what I want, no possible computer can derive my utility function since it does not
really exist."[29]

EXPERT: That's correct. As I remember it, Buchanan
never did consider the theory of choice central to the
study of economic theory.

ATTORNEY: And hasn't F. A. Hayek, another Nobel laureate in economics, criticized your profession for
what he calls its "abuse of reason," its penchant for
engaging in "scientism," and its failure to recognize
that imperfect knowledge is endemic to the human
condition? Hasn't he derided economists for aping
the methods of the physical sciences, mindlessly
misapplying them to socioeconomic phenomena,
and reaching absurd conclusions as a result?[30]

[29] James Buchanan, *What Should Economists Do?* (Indianapolis: Liberty
Press, 1979), 25–26. See also Harvey Leibenstein, *Beyond Economic Man*
(Cambridge: Harvard University Press, 1976).

Herbert A. Simon, another Nobel laureate in economics and founding
father of artificial intelligence, warns that "any model of human behavior
that focuses on decision making gives us an overrational idea of humans."
After all, he says, "one doesn't spend most of one's time making decisions.
One lives. I don't feel like I'm in a maze." "The choices we make lead up
to actual experiences," he explains. "It is one thing to decide to climb a
mountain. It is quite another to be on top of it." Interview, *New York
Times Book Review*, Mar. 17, 1991, 29.

[30] See F. A. Hayek, *The Counter-Revolution of Science: Studies in the
Abuse of Reason* (Glencoe, Ill.: Free Press, 1952), 14–16, 30, 51; and Hayek's Nobel Memorial Lecture, "The Pretense of Knowledge," reprinted in
American Economic Review 79 (Dec. 1989): 3. For a related criticism of
what G. Warren Nutter has characterized as "economism"—that is, the
universal application of economic theory to the analysis of *all* human behavior and social activity—see G. Warren Nutter, "On Economism," *Journal of Law and Economics* 22 (Oct. 1979): 263–68.

EXPERT: So he has.

ATTORNEY: And hasn't the illustrious Frank Knight—
your teacher at Chicago—warned economists against
trying to ape the methodology of the natural sciences? Hasn't he pointed out that "the fundamental
revolution and outlook which represents the real be-
ginning of modern natural science was the discovery
that the inert objects of nature are not like men, that
is, subject to persuasion, exhortation, coercion, de-
ception, etc., but are 'inexorable' "? Hasn't he ad-
monished economists to combat the inference "that
since natural objects are not like men, men must be
like natural objects"?[31]

EXPERT: I am quite cognizant of Knight's cautionary
counsel.

ATTORNEY: In your reliance on the rational choice
model, aren't you underestimating the substantial
role of nonpurposive, nonrational behavior? Everyone would agree that there is an element of *Homo
economicus* in every individual, but how do you explain the behavior of the romantic fool, the person
who enjoys the fray, the prejudiced ignoramus?[32]
Conceding the fact that some individuals are rational maximizers of economic interest, aren't there
other types—the Malthusian consumer, the martyr,
the patriot, the ideologue, the addict, the fanatic,
etc.?[33]

---

[31] Frank Knight, *On the History and Method of Economics* (Chicago:
University of Chicago Press, 1956), 121–22.

[32] Buchanan, Foreword to Frank Knight, *Freedom and Reform* (Indianapolis: Liberty Press, 1982), xii.

[33] Nutter, "On Economism," 263, 265.

EXPERT: Be that as it may, the heart of the economic approach is to rely, relentlessly and unflinchingly, on the combined assumptions of maximizing behavior, market equilibrium, and stable preferences.[34]

ATTORNEY: I guess it's futile to pursue this point. But I cannot resist reminding you of Alexander Pope's poetic advice: "Be sure yourself and your own reach to know/How far your genius, taste, and learning go/ Launch not beyond your depth; but be discreet/And mark that point where sense and dullness meet."[35]

EXPERT: Pope has never been one of my favorites. I much prefer the nineteenth-century British romantics—Byron, Keats, Shelley, etc.

ATTORNEY: I trust you will spare us an economic interpretation of their poetry.

The Testimony on the Application of Price Theory to Antitrust

EXPERT: To be serious again, I will agree that much of economics is vague. When applied to antitrust, however, microeconomics is not vague. It is quite powerful.[36]

ATTORNEY: All right, then, let us turn to antitrust. What is the relevance of price theory to antitrust?

[34] Becker, *Economic Approach to Human Behavior*, 5.

[35] Alexander Pope, "An Essay on Criticism," reprinted in *Pope: Poems* (New York: Viking Press, 1985), 15.

[36] Robert H. Bork, "Judicial Precedent and the New Economics," in Eleanor Fox and J. Halverson, eds., *Antitrust Policy in Transition: The Convergence of Law and Economics* (Chicago: American Bar Association, 1984), 16.

EXPERT: Antitrust is about the effects of business behavior on consumers. To understand the impact of
business behavior on consumer well-being we are
forced to rely on basic economic theory. This should
not be worrisome, because the economic models essential to antitrust analysis are simple and don't require any previous training in economics.[37]

ATTORNEY: And price theory is robust enough to measure up to this task?

EXPERT: Basic price theory is an intensely logical subject. It is such a powerful explanatory tool that we
can be certain, or virtually certain, of its reliability.[38]

ATTORNEY: Does it not make you uneasy to rely entirely upon a theory to infer the nature of a reality
that is not directly observed?

EXPERT: I am convinced that the theory is good enough
to make the task doable. I am also convinced that
there is no other possible way to get the job done.[39]
Indeed, unless we rely on economic theory, we cannot possibly have a rational antitrust law.[40]

ATTORNEY: What do you consider a rational antitrust
law?

EXPERT: Professor Bork has said it best: "The law's mission is to preserve, improve, and reinforce the powerful economic mechanisms that compel businesses
to respond to consumers."[41] The main—indeed, the

---

[37] Robert Bork, *The Antitrust Paradox* (New York: Basic Books, 1978),
90.
[38] Ibid., 117.
[39] Ibid., 122.
[40] Ibid., 117.
[41] Ibid., 91.

exclusive—concern of antitrust is the maximization
of consumer welfare.

ATTORNEY: Are you using the term "consumer welfare"
in the vernacular sense—in Ralph Nader's sense?

EXPERT: No, in the scientific sense—in the Pareto opti-
mality sense.

ATTORNEY: Would you tell us what that means, please?

EXPERT: General welfare is at a maximum when no one
can be made better off without making someone else
worse off.

ATTORNEY: By that standard, how is consumer welfare
maximized?

EXPERT: Consumer welfare is maximized when society's economic resources are allocated so that consumer wants are satisfied as fully as technological
constraints permit. Simply put, consumer welfare is
the measure of a nation's wealth.[42]

ATTORNEY: Is this what economists call allocative efficiency?

EXPERT: Yes. It is to be distinguished from productive
efficiency, which consists of the effective use of resources by individual firms.

ATTORNEY: How does a laissez-faire policy help to
achieve allocative efficiency, or maximum consumer
welfare?

EXPERT: In a market economy, the profit motive is
given free reign. Producers must earn profits if they
are to survive. They are in constant search for them.
In a market economy, the pursuit of profit is pat-

[42] Ibid., 90.

ently ubiquitous and overwhelming.[43] Therefore producers will use society's resources to make things and provide services that consumers want, because that is the only way of earning profits.

ATTORNEY: Are you saying that businesspeople are motivated solely, or even primarily, by the search for profit?

EXPERT: Business people don't always talk in terms of profit maximization, but that is of no particular significance.[44] For purposes of the theory, it is enough if they generally behave *as if* they were engaged in profit maximization. As Milton Friedman, a Nobel laureate in economics, has pointed out, "[F]irms behave *as if* they were seeking rationally to maximize their expected returns . . . and had full knowledge of the data required to do so; *as if*, that is, they knew the relevant cost and demand functions, calculated marginal cost and marginal revenue from all actions open to them, and pushed each line of action to the point at which the relevant marginal cost and marginal revenue were equal."[45]

ATTORNEY: Let us come back to consumer welfare. Are you saying that producers' search for profit will automatically ensure that consumers will get what they want?

EXPERT: Consumers make choices that they believe will maximize their individual well-being. Firms, in their own self-interest, will then strive to satisfy

[43] Ibid., 119.
[44] Ibid., 121.
[45] Milton Friedman, "The Methodology of Positive Economics," in William Breit and Harold M. Hochman, eds., *Readings in Microeconomics* (New York: Holt, Rinehart & Winston, 1968), 34–35.

those choices. This process will work as the theory predicts, except where it is short-circuited by cartels or monopolies.

ATTORNEY: How can we be sure that firms will produce the kinds of goods consumers actually want?

EXPERT: There is one simple test. If consumers don't want those goods, they won't buy them. The fact that they do buy them proves that consumers are getting what they want—that their welfare is being served.

ATTORNEY: But what if consumer choice is artificially restricted? For example, for three decades Detroit's Big Three offered only large, gas-guzzling cars, which consumers bought. Does this prove that gas guzzlers maximized consumer welfare—even though consumers might have preferred to buy smaller, fuel-efficient cars if they had been made available? Didn't this restricted range of choice—choose any car so long as it is a gas guzzler—make the consumer a choice *taker* rather than a choice *maker*?

EXPERT: If consumers didn't want gas guzzlers, they wouldn't buy them. If they preferred smaller, fuel-efficient cars, new firms would come into the market to make them available. The fact that this doesn't happen proves that consumers are content with the range of choices open to them.

ATTORNEY: But what if, for example, the Big Three succeed in blocking entry of small, fuel-efficient cars by persuading Washington to impose tariffs, quotas, or other barriers against foreign producers anxious to sell such cars in the U.S. market and thus expand the options available to American consumers?

EXPERT: That is a political problem—the interference by the state with free market forces.

ATTORNEY: In the real world, can we separate political influence from economic power? Isn't this why Adam Smith chose to talk about political economy rather than economics narrowly defined? Didn't he demonstrate in lurid detail the dangers to the public of tolerating the coalescence between economic and political power?

EXPERT: So he did, and that is why laissez-faire economists are intent on limiting the role of government to a bare minimum.

ATTORNEY: Let's see whether I understand your argument. Are you saying that whatever consumers choose is "efficient" because it maximizes their utility, and whatever firms produce maximizes consumer welfare? Are you saying that if this were not so, different choices would be made? Are you saying that the fact that different choices are not made proves that the actual choices reflect a voluntary, noncoerced optimum of consumer welfare—that it proves that the current pattern of resource use reflects maximum allocative efficiency of the system?

EXPERT: Yes, except for any distortions caused by cartels or monopolies.

ATTORNEY: Isn't your argument tautological—a species of circular reasoning?

EXPERT: Not at all. It describes how a free market system works. As Judge Bork so aptly put it, "Microeconomic theory rests upon a few empirical premises. For example, other things being equal more of a product is demanded as price falls. That is an empirical proposition that nobody has ever successfully rebutted. Once a few such basic premises are accepted, the rest follows like a proof in geometry. The system is entirely circular, which is its strength because circular logic is not rebuttable."[46]

ATTORNEY: You make it sound as if economists, armed with price theory, can explain anything.[47] Most people, I submit, would consider your claims for price theory extravagant and extreme. Some might even regard the theory as a fable—like the tooth fairy or the Easter bunny or Santa Claus.

EXPERT: That may be your opinion. But it's a fact that not only economists but judges, attorneys, Washington administrators, and public policymakers are increasingly embracing the New Learning. Indeed, the ascendancy of the New Learning now seems all but inevitable.[48]

ATTORNEY: I can't resist asking: If the world works as rationally and as perfectly as you claim it does, what need is there for economists like yourself?

EXPERT: Obviously to prevent naive people from implementing foolish economic policies.

---

[46] Statement in Fox and Halverson, *Antitrust Policy in Transition.*

[47] James Buchanan offers this note of caution: "[E]conomic theory can, of course, explain everything, but this is familiarly equivalent to saying that it predicts nothing." Buchanan, *What Should Economists Do?* 78–79.

[48] James C. Miller III, *The Economist as Reformer* (Washington, D.C.: American Enterprise Institute, 1989), 47. For a contrary opinion, see Herbert Hovenkamp, "Antitrust Policy after Chicago," *University of Michigan Law Review* 94 (1985): 213. Hovenkamp argues that "flaws in the Chicago model's basic premises will one day cause it to be eclipsed, just as previously ascendant doctrines have been eclipsed" (p. 213). Frederick Rowe made the same point in "The Decline of Antitrust and the Delusion of Models: The Faustian Pact of Law and Economics," *Georgetown Law Journal* 72 (1984): 1511.

ATTORNEY: Fair enough. Let us return to the role of antitrust. You've quoted Robert Bork's statement that "the law's mission is to preserve, improve, and reinforce the powerful economic mechanisms that compel businesses to respond to consumers." Specifically what does that imply?

EXPERT: It requires the suppression of cartels and monopolies—that is, the types of behavior that restrict output and raise price.

ATTORNEY: Am I correct in assuming that there is near-unanimity among economists that cartel-like restrictions of output and collusion in pricing have antisocial consequences?

EXPERT: That is correct. Professor (now Judge) Richard Posner, for example, would even go so far as to forbid tacit as well as overt collusion. He feels that in some oligopoly cases, juries should be instructed to find an agreement to fix prices if there was a tacit meeting of the minds among the defendants on maintaining a noncompetitive pricing policy. To be sure, Posner recognizes that there are dangers in pressing the "meeting-of-minds" approach too far.[49]

ATTORNEY: But does this make sense? Isn't the essence of oligopoly behavior a recognition of mutual interdependence, and does this not militate toward tacit collusion? Would a rule prohibiting such collusion in oligopoly markets require oligopolists to behave irrationally in order to comply with the law?[50]

---

[49] Richard A. Posner, *Antitrust Law* (Chicago: University of Chicago Press, 1976), 72.

[50] See Donald Turner, "The Definition of Agreement under the Sherman Act: Conscious Parallelism and Refusals to Deal," *Harvard Law Review* 75 (1962): 655, 669.

EXPERT: No. Oligopoly may be a necessary condition for tacit collusion, but it is not a sufficient condition.

ATTORNEY: Be that as it may, what is the major vice of monopoly as you see it?

EXPERT: Let me refer you to Exhibit 1—the chart on the easel next to the jury box. That graph demonstrates the social losses as well as the potential gains from monopoly and mergers of monopolistic dimensions.

ATTORNEY: Please explain.

EXPERT: Assume that Q_1 represents a "competitive" output and P_1 a "competitive" price. A rational monopolist (following the profit-maximizing rule of operating where marginal cost equals marginal revenue) will restrict output to Q_2 and raise price to P_2. The result is a "dead weight" loss to consumers—a diminution of consumer welfare—measured by the area of triangle A_1.

ATTORNEY: And the rectangle labeled A_2?

EXHIBIT 1. EFFECT OF MONOPOLY ON OUTPUT (Q), PRICE (P), AND AVERAGE COST (AC)

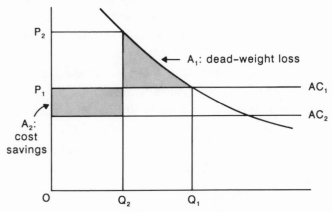

EXPERT: That represents average cost under competitive conditions (AC₁) minus a monopoly's average cost (AC₂). Thus it measures the cost savings—the increases in "production" efficiency—that are attributable to the existence of monopoly or result from the consummation of a monopolistic merger. In order to ascertain the net effect on consumer welfare, we would have to compare the size of A_1 and A_2.

ATTORNEY: Would your graph also be relevant to an assessment of oligopoly?

EXPERT: Yes, to the extent that the oligopoly practices overt or tacit collusion.

ATTORNEY: Are you suggesting that this graph accurately depicts what antitrust is all about?

EXPERT: Yes, but care must be taken in applying it to actual cases. We shouldn't condemn monopoly out of hand.

ATTORNEY: Please elaborate.

EXPERT: It would be easy to jump to the conclusion that the process of natural selection doesn't work in a market dominated by a single-firm monopoly or a market where the entry of newcomers is blocked. Even in this situation, however, consumer welfare is not *necessarily* diminished. The monopolistic firm would still have the incentive to *simulate* the struggle for survival by trying to minimize its cost and hence maximize its profits. It would still strive to make the area of rectangle A_2 on our graph as large as possible, and this would benefit consumer welfare and efficiency as I have defined it.[51]

---

[51] Posner, *Antitrust Law*, 16.

JUDGE: Wait a moment. [*To the witness*] As I listen to your answer, it seems to me that your interpretation of competition is compatible with a completely monopolized economy. Isn't there a rather serious contradiction here?

EXPERT: Not at all, Your Honor. As Judge Posner points out, we value competition in economic affairs because it promotes efficiency—that is, we value competition as a means, rather than an end. Thus, if monopoly would increase efficiency, monopoly should be tolerated—indeed, encouraged.[52]

ATTORNEY: [*Resuming the examination*] But would the benefit of this increased efficiency—a larger A_2—be passed on to consumers in the form of lower prices?

EXPERT: The answer is yes, because in the long run a market position that creates output restriction and higher prices will always be vulnerable. It is certain to be eroded unless, of course, it is based upon superior efficiency.[53]

ATTORNEY: What do you mean by the long run? The courts declared that Kodak possessed an unlawful monopoly as long ago as 1916, and more than fifty years later Kodak still exercised dominant control over the amateur photography market. Apparently the long run can be quite long in some cases.

EXPERT: Undoubtedly, the long run is longer in some cases than in others. But recall that in such cases, the persistence of monopoly must be based on supe-

---

[52] Ibid., 22. For a critique of this view, see Rudolph J. Peritz, "A Counter-History of Antitrust Law," *Duke Law Journal* (1990): 263–320. For an analogy of the Posner analysis to a picaresque novel, see Arthur A. Leff, "Economic Analysis of Law," *Virginia Law Review* 60 (1974): 451.

[53] Bork, *Antitrust Paradox*, 133.

rior efficiency—what Judge Learned Hand called "superior skill, foresight, and industry."[54] A history of absence of entry in an industry with a high concentration index may be a sign of virtue, not of vice.[55]

ATTORNEY: How can you be sure of that? Has not Professor George Stigler, a Nobel laureate, demonstrated that most giant firms have been the artificial creature of mergers and acquisitions rather than the result of internal growth based on superior performance? Hasn't Stigler shown that monopoly-sized firms are neither inevitable nor dictated by economic efficiency?[56]

The Testimony on the Contestable Market Theory

EXPERT: If a monopolist's position were not due to superior efficiency, its market share would be eroded by the entry of new firms. The only way the monopolist can prevent such entry is by performing well— that is, by acting in ways that offer consumers all the benefits that competition would generate if it existed. Any deviation from good performance instantly renders the monopolist vulnerable to hit-and-run market entry by competitors. This is what the theory of contestable markets teaches us.[57]

[54] United States v. Aluminum Co. of America, 148 F.2d 416, (1945).

[55] William J. Baumol, "Contestable Markets: An Uprising in the Theory of Industry Structure," American Economic Review 72 (Mar. 1982): 14.

[56] George Stigler, "The Case against Big Business," Fortune, May 1952, 162; id., "Monopoly and Oligopoly by Merger," American Economic Review 40 (May 1950): 23.

[57] Baumol, "Contestable Markets," 14.

ATTORNEY: Would you explain the contestable market theory?

EXPERT: It is a generalization of the theory of perfect competition. A perfectly contestable market is characterized by optimal behavior and can exist within a full range of industry structures, including even monopoly and oligopoly.[58] The analysis vastly extends the domain of the invisible hand.[59] It shows that even in highly concentrated markets, the price, in equilibrium, must be exactly equal to marginal cost (as it would be under perfect competition), and that resource allocation will be optimal.[60]

ATTORNEY: Why would that be so?

EXPERT: Because potential entry into or competition *for* the market disciplines behavior almost as effectively as would actual competition *within* the market. Thus, even if a market is dominated by a single firm, it is contestable and will perform in a competitive fashion.[61]

---

[58] Ibid., 2.

[59] Ibid.

[60] Ibid., 5. For a comprehensive critique of this theory, see William G. Shepherd, " 'Contestability' versus Competition," *American Economic Review* 74 (1984): 572–87.

[61] Elizabeth Bailey, "Contestability and the Design of Regulatory and Antitrust Policy," *American Economic Review* 71 (May 1981): 178. An interesting endorsement of the contestable market theory is to be found in the apparently serious effort by a Chinese commentator to apply the New Learning to the role of mistresses in Communist China: "The introduction of the mechanism of competition into the economy has drastically transformed our society in a few short years. People don't deny the usefulness of competition simply because a few factories have gone under. Similarly, we should also be advocating competition in marriage and the 'third person' would provide just such a competitive force. If society allowed this sort of competition to exist, the two parties to a marriage are bound to feel that without constant hard work the threat of the 'third person' always lurks nearby." *New York Times*, June 4, 1988, 4.

ATTORNEY: Are you saying that it makes no difference whether the structure of a market is competitive or monopolistic?

EXPERT: Yes, markets need not be atomistic to be competitive or to perform well.[62]

ATTORNEY: Let me pose a hypothetical. Take the domestic airline industry, for example. Is it not true that the series of megamergers following deregulation and the concomitant increase in concentration resulted in significant fare increases and noticeable deterioration of service? After acquiring Ozark, for example, TWA discontinued forty flights out of St. Louis, and raised fares by as much as 33 percent. At eighteen hubs where a single airline controls 50 percent or more of the traffic, originating passengers are forced to pay significantly higher fares—in some cases over 50 percent more—compared to standard levels. How can you deny that as dominant carriers carve up the country into regional monopolies, the flying public pays more and more for less and less?[63]

EXPERT: The purpose of deregulation is to allow free market forces to determine the best economic organization of the industry. Whenever and wherever there is a profitable opportunity in a deregulated airline market, an entrant need merely fly its airplane into the airport, undercut the incumbent's price, and fly the route profitably. Should the incumbent retal-

[62] Miller, The Economist As Reformer, 47.
[63] Walter Adams and James W. Brock, Dangerous Pursuits: Mergers and Acquisitions in the Age of Wall Street (New York: Pantheon Books, 1989), 105.

iate with a sharp price cut, the entrepreneur will fly its airplane away to exploit some other lucrative opportunity. Clearly, air travel provides one concrete example of contestable markets. And, clearly, the reversible potential entry of contestable markets is consistent with maximal welfare.[64]

ATTORNEY: Is it your contention that potential entrants can freely fly into lucrative markets and erode the monopoly or oligopoly power of incumbent carriers?

EXPERT: Yes. In the absence of regulatory intervention, aviation markets are naturally contestable. That's because the major portion of airline capital costs, the aircraft, can readily be moved from one market to another.[65]

ATTORNEY: Where are the potential entrants going to obtain landing gates at overcrowded airports, such as O'Hare, Kennedy, or Los Angeles?

EXPERT: They can buy gates from carriers who currently own them.

ATTORNEY: In other words, from the very companies whose market power the entrant is trying to undermine. And are you suggesting that these companies would cheerfully cooperate?

EXPERT: They might, if the price were attractive enough. Besides, the problem could easily be solved by expanding crowded airports. That would alleviate the present scarcity of gates.

---

[64] William J. Baumol, John C. Panzar, and Robert D. Willig, *Contestable Markets and the Theory of Industry Structure* (San Diego: Harcourt, Brace, Jovanovich, 1982), 7–8.

[65] Bailey, "Contestability and the Design of Regulatory and Antitrust Policy," 179–80.

ATTORNEY: And what about the reservations systems now controlled by the dominant airlines? How is the potential entrant to gain access to these systems, which are crucial to its survival?

EXPERT: By paying for it or by developing its own reservation system.

ATTORNEY: Obviously this means raising the cost of entry and making the possibility of new competition more remote.

EXPERT: The assumption that entry into a monopolist's or a cartel's market can be blocked is quite unrealistic.[66] No good explanation has ever been provided to demonstrate how present and potential rivals are kept from competing without some government-imposed restriction on competitive activities.[67] Concentrated markets that yield above-average profits can remain concentrated only if they are protected by government[68] or by predation—or if they exhibit superior efficiency.

The Testimony on the Predation "Problem"

ATTORNEY: Would you tell us what you mean by "predation"?

EXPERT: Yes. Predation may be defined as a form of aggression against one's rivals. It is launched not to increase the predator's profits, but in the expectation

---

[66] Posner, *Antitrust Law*, 17.

[67] Harold Demsetz, "Two Systems of Belief about Monopoly," in Goldschmid, Mann, and Weston, eds., *Industrial Concentration: The New Learning* (Boston: Little, Brown & Co., 1974), 166–67.

[68] Demsetz, "Two Systems of Belief About Monopoly," 168.

either that its rivals will be driven from the market, leaving the predator with a market share sufficient to command monopoly profits, or that the rivals will be chastened sufficiently to forsake competitive behavior.[69]

ATTORNEY: From a scientific point of view, do you consider such predation to be a legitimate problem, meriting antitrust attention?

EXPERT: It is dubious on theoretical grounds.[70]

ATTORNEY: Why is that?

EXPERT: Because in theory, predatory pricing requires the predator to bear losses that are much larger than those inflicted on the intended victim.[71] Since the predator already has a proportionately larger share of the market, it will suffer proportionately larger losses as a result of its predation.

ATTORNEY: But couldn't the predator engage in "sharpshooting" predation, by narrowly tailoring its price cuts to the particular regions and locales where an upstart threatens to compete, while leaving unaltered its prices in the remainder of its markets?

EXPERT: The belief that a multimarket firm can engage in predation by lowering its prices to uneconomic levels in one market and compensate for the costs of predation by raising its prices elsewhere is a foolish theory.[72]

ATTORNEY: Why do you consider that to be a foolish theory?

[69] Bork, *Antitrust Paradox*, 144.
[70] Federal Trade Commission Transition Report, prepared for President Reagan, reprinted in *Congressional Record* (Senate), Sept. 21, 1981, 21350.
[71] Bork, *Antitrust Paradox*, 148.
[72] Ibid., 144–45.

EXPERT: Because it rests upon the foolish recoupment fallacy. Economic theory dictates that the alleged predator would already be maximizing its profits in *all* of its markets. From which markets, therefore, would it get the additional profits to finance predation? Recoupment is a theoretical impossibility even if the predator enjoys a monopoly position in some markets.[73]

ATTORNEY: But in the airline industry, for example, isn't there rather well-documented evidence that the dominant carriers have used selective, targeted and sharp price cuts to eliminate or discipline smaller carriers in particular city-pair markets, without having to cut fares throughout their entire systems? And isn't it a fact that such discriminatory pricing has played an important role in the demise of smaller, independent carriers as a source of potential competition against the airline oligopoly?[74]

---

[73] Ibid., 145.
[74] Alfred E. Kahn, "Thinking about Predation: A Personal Diary" (Paper delivered at Conference on Appraisal of the Sherman Act: 1890–1990, Michigan State University, Sept. 7, 1990).

A recent front-page *Wall Street Journal* article examining airline pricing reported:

"The most common—and perhaps most questionable— 'discussion' between airlines is played out like this: Carrier A—often a smaller operator such as Midway Airlines or America West—attempts to boost its business by lowering ticket prices. It enters lower fares in the industry's computer system. In response, Carrier B—the dominant carrier at the affected airport —not only matches the new fares, but lowers them in other markets that are served by carrier A.

"Carrier B may also attach special codes to its new fares to get its message across. Pricing executives say some carriers have been known to prefix new fares with the letters 'FU' to indicate an indelicate imperative. The end result is that Carrier B often cancels its reduction, depriving consumers of a lower fare." Asra Nomani, "Airlines May Be Using a Price-Data Network to Lessen Competition," *Wall Street Journal*, June 28, 1990, A6.

EXPERT: An abundance of unsophisticated theories drastically exaggerate the likelihood of predation.[75]

ATTORNEY: Why do you characterize these as unsophisticated?

EXPERT: Because they naively assume that a large firm somehow has enough raw power to beat smaller firms to death.[76]

ATTORNEY: But in cable television, to take another example, doesn't experience show that when new firms have attempted to compete, incumbent local monopolies have responded by slashing rates sharply, or have even provided some services free of charge to residents in the cities where a new firm is attempting to compete while, at the same time, raising service prices in their monopoly territories?[77] Doesn't this indicate that, contrary to your claim, large incumbent firms can, in fact, "beat" smaller firms into submission?

EXPERT: An uninformed sort of super–Queensbury rules attitude persists about the nature of the competitive

---

In another article, the *Wall Street Journal* reported:

"A few weeks ago, Braniff sprang a surprise on some of its airline rivals: It slashed prices for off-peak travel in 43 markets.

"The very next day, Continental Airlines struck back. Irked that some of the Braniff cuts were aimed at its Houston hub, Continental, a unit of Texas Air Corp., retaliated by cutting selected fares out of Kansas City— Braniff's home turf.

"Last Thursday, Braniff caved in under the pressure. The unit of BIA-COR Holdings Inc. ended its special discounts." Nomani, "Dispatches from the Air-Fare Front," *Wall Street Journal*, July 11, 1989, B1.

[75] Bork, *Antitrust Paradox*, 144.

[76] Ibid.

[77] In re Competition, Rate Regulation and the Commission's Policies Relating to the Provision of Cable Television Service: Comments of Telesat Cablevision Inc. to the Federal Communications Commission, MM Docket No. 89–600 (Mar. 1, 1990), 20–23.

process—an attitude espoused by courts in earlier years. But what you call predation is nothing more than the kind of good, hard competition that the antitrust laws are intended to promote in a free market. Thus, the great majority of predation allegations are without economic substance.[78]

ATTORNEY: Isn't it also a fact that Anheuser-Busch, the nation's largest beer brewer, recently used the threat of sharp price cuts to discipline smaller firms in the industry and to dissuade them from price competition? Is it not the case that rather than cutting its prices in all of its markets, Busch cut them in fewer than a third of its markets, while making few price changes in less competitive markets—and that as a result, according to *Business Week*, Busch is "keeping the peace by raising the cost of war"?[79] And don't consumers pay higher prices as a result?

EXPERT: According to modern economic theory, your argument is tantamount to saying that a man

---

[78] Interview with William F. Baxter, Assistant Attorney General, Antitrust Division, Department of Justice, *Antitrust Law Journal* 52 (1983): 23, 27.

[79] Julia Siler, "A Warning Shot from the King of Beers," *Business Week*, Dec. 18, 1989, 124. See also N. R. Kleinfield, "The King of Beers Raises the Ante," *New York Times*, Dec. 24, 1989, sec. 3, p. 1.

For similar evidence regarding the efforts of the major cigarette producers to drive a producer of low-priced "generic" cigarettes from the field, see Stephen Adler and Alix Freedman, "Tobacco Suit Exposes Ways Cigarette Firms Keep the Profits Fat," *Wall Street Journal*, March 5, 1990, A1. This article reported that "B & W was prepared, according to its documents, to lose money on the generics in order to stem the tide of smokers defecting from its name brands. 'L&M will attempt to retain this business but lacks financial strength to cover all fronts on a sustained basis,' one B & W planning document predicted" (p. A5).

For a comprehensive study of predation in the Canadian telecommunication industry, see Robert E. Babe, *Telecommunications in Canada* (Toronto: University of Toronto Press, 1990), esp. chs. 12 and 13.

jumped out of a window and fell upwards.[80] I have explained as clearly as I can how economic theory deduces that predatory price cutting is most unlikely to exist, and that attempts to outlaw it are likely to harm consumers.[81]

ATTORNEY: But is it not a fact that in a 1988 case the Second Circuit Court of Appeals found that one of the largest trash-hauling firms in the industry, Browning-Ferris, decided to " '[p]ut a [new competitor] out of business. Do whatever it takes. Squish him like a bug' "; if " 'it meant giv[ing services] away, give [them] away.' " This was followed by a 40 percent slash in prices—to a level substantially below the firm's costs?[82]

EXPERT: Such a tactic is theoretically improbable.[83]

ATTORNEY: Why is that?

EXPERT: Because by depressing the value of the victim's business, the predator makes that business an attractive investment for other competitors, rendering predation pointless.[84]

ATTORNEY: But doesn't the actual occurence of such predation serve as a warning to any future potential entrant, thereby deterring new firms from entering the market and absorbing such losses all over again?[85] Having witnessed such predation in the

[80] Bork, "Judicial Precedent," 16.
[81] Bork, *Antitrust Paradox*, 155.
[82] Kelco Disposal v. Browning-Ferris Industries, 845 F.2d 404, 406 (2d Cir. 1988).
[83] Bork, *Antitrust Paradox*, 153.
[84] Ibid.
[85] After reviewing the evidence that scores of smaller competitors have been predatorily driven from the airline industry by the dominant incumbent carriers and that "the likelihood of imitators following their lead is

past, would the capital markets really be willing to finance a similar venture in the future?

EXPERT: It is common to hear objections that the victim will not be able to find outside capital because the capital market is imperfect. It is not evidence of imperfection if a lender refuses to make an unprofitable loan.[86]

ATTORNEY: Well then, on the basis of your economic theory, what do you conclude is the theoretically correct antitrust policy toward predatory pricing?

EXPERT: Predatory pricing has become part of the antitrust folklore.[87] It seems unwise to construct rules about a phenomenon that probably does not exist.[88]

ATTORNEY: And what is your opinion of predatory practices—such as impeding rivals' access to inputs, facilities, or distribution channels—which enable a dominant firm to undercut competition by raising the costs of its rivals?[89]

EXPERT: I repeat: The central problem with any policy against predation is the conceptual difficulty of distinguishing competition from predation. For this reason, I conclude that there is no justification

---

surely nil, or close to it," economist Alfred Kahn concludes: "The single greatest obstacle to entry [in the airline industry] is not hub domination but the certainty that any such direct competitive challenge would be met immediately, selectively, and hard. . . ." Alfred Kahn, "Thinking about Predation," 7, 11.

[86] Bork, *Antitrust Paradox*, 147–48.

[87] Thomas DiLorenzo, "The Rhetoric of Antitrust," Center for the Study of American Business Contemporary Issue Series no. 22 (St. Louis: CSAB, Nov. 1986), 9.

[88] Bork, *Antitrust Paradox*, 154.

[89] See Thomas G. Krattenmaker and Stephen C. Salop, "Anticompetitive Exclusion: Raising Rivals' Costs to Achieve Power over Price," *Yale Law Journal* 96 (Dec. 1986): 209–93.

for antitrust law or the courts to take predation seriously.[90]

The Testimony on Superior Efficiency and the Persistence of Monopoly

ATTORNEY: Let me come back to your statements on efficiency. In your testimony, you have repeatedly claimed that the persistence of monopoly or oligopoly is, in the absence of government protection, attributable to superior efficiency and hence compatible with efforts to maximize consumer welfare. What evidence do you have to support this claim?

EXPERT: I believe that the ultimate facts relevant for antitrust purposes cannot be perceived directly. Nor can they be scientifically quantified. So-called performance tests and efficiency defenses are spurious. They cannot measure the factors relevant to consumer welfare; thus, after the extravaganza of an economic investigation was completed, we wouldn't know any more than we did before it began.[91]

ATTORNEY: Why not?

EXPERT: It is impossible to determine whether there exists in a particular industry a persistent divergence between price and marginal cost; the precise extent of the divergence; whether the divergence could be

[90] Frank H. Easterbrook, "Predatory Strategies and Counterstrategies," *University of Chicago Law Review* 48 (1986): 246, 333. For an alternative analysis, see James W. Brock, "Structural Monopoly, Technological Performance, and Predatory Innovation: Relevant Standards Under Section 2 of the Sherman Act," *American Business Law Journal* 21 (Fall 1983): 291–306.

[91] Bork, *Antitrust Paradox*, 124–25.

reduced or eliminated by breaking up, say, four firms into eight, or eight firms into sixteen; and whether any significant efficiencies would be destroyed if we undertook such a structural reorganization.[92]

ATTORNEY: Wouldn't it be possible to make a passably accurate measurement of an actual situation?

EXPERT: That is not even a theoretical possibility; moreover, there isn't much chance of making a correct estimate in a *hypothetical* situation.[93]

ATTORNEY: Why not?

EXPERT: Consider two of the factors that would have to be known: the demand curve and the marginal cost curve over all possibly relevant ranges of output. Only if we knew where marginal cost and demand intersect could we determine whether there was a restriction of output and whether it was significant.[94]

ATTORNEY: Are you saying that it is impossible to come by this information?

EXPERT: Yes. Nobody, not even the companies involved, knows these curves. The clarity of the graphs describing firm behavior misleads many people.[95]

ATTORNEY: If the graphs—like the one we have examined earlier—are misleading, what guides does management follow in making its day-to-day and long-range decisions?

EXPERT: Management may never think of the curves shown on our graph. It may think in terms of a fair return and average costs, but competition and the de-

[92] Ibid., 125.
[93] Ibid.
[94] Ibid., 126–27.
[95] Ibid., 126.

sire to maximize profit will push management to the solution shown on the graph.[96]

ATTORNEY: Hasn't Professor Joe S. Bain of the University of California succeeded in estimating efficiency on both the plant and the firm level in twenty representative industries in the United States?[97] Hasn't Professor F. M. Scherer of Harvard's Kennedy School of Government made a similar attempt in a massive cross-sectional, cross-national empirical study?[98]

EXPERT: These studies and others like them are fatally flawed because they try to measure only engineering or technological efficiency. They leave out of account such crucial components of efficiency as marketing efficiencies, financial efficiencies, managerial efficiencies, etc. Skepticism should turn to utter disbelief at the sight of a cost curve purporting to reflect all these efficiencies.[99]

JUDGE: [To the witness] Hold on a moment! What does that leave us with in terms of empirical evidence?

[96] Ibid.

[97] In his definitive study of twenty representative industries, Joe S. Bain found that in eleven out of twenty cases, the lowest-cost (most efficient) plant accounted for less than 2.5 percent of the industry's national sales; in fifteen out of twenty cases, for less than 7.5 percent; and in only one case, for more than 15 percent. Moreover, in estimating multiplant economies, Bain concluded that in six out of twenty industries, the cost advantages of multiplant firms were "either negligible or totally absent"; in another six industries, the advantages were "perceptible" but "fairly small"; and in the remaining eight industries, no estimate could be obtained. Joe S. Bain, *Barriers to New Competition* (Cambridge: Harvard University Press, 1956), 73 and 85–88ff. These findings hardly support the contention that existing concentration in American industry can be explained in terms of technological imperatives.

[98] F. M Scherer et al., *The Economics of Multi-Plant Operation: An International Comparisons Study* (Cambridge: Harvard University Press, 1975).

[99] Bork, *Antitrust Paradox*, 127.

On what basis am I, and other judges, to decide concrete cases? On the basis of abstract economic theory or on the facts of a particular case?

EXPERT: Well, we have to trust the theory and rely on common sense.[100] We just have to recognize that economists, like other scientists, tend to measure what is measurable and forget about the rest, even though what is not measured may be vastly more important than what is measured.[101]

ATTORNEY: [*Resuming the examination*] All right, then. Let us review your testimony up to this point. You've stated that modern microeconomic theory— what some like to call the New Learning—is a science that explains not only economic behavior but human behavior generally.

EXPERT: That is correct.

ATTORNEY: You maintain that the core concern of antitrust is to promote consumer welfare, which you equate with allocative efficiency—that is, the "aggregate consumer willingness to pay for goods and services."[102]

EXPERT: Correct.

---

[100] Posner, *Antitrust Law*, 91. In a comprehensive review of the Chicago school, Melvin W. Reder (a Chicago alumnus) criticizes this methodology. In most scientific endeavors, Reder writes, it is customary to confront theory with evidence. By contrast, "Chicago economists tend strongly to appraise their own research and that of others by a standard which requires (inter alia) that the findings of empirical research be consistent with the implications of standard price theory." Melvin W. Reder, "Chicago Economics: Permanence and Change," *Journal of Economic Literature* 20 (1982): 13. If evidence arises that appears to conflict with their tight prior equilibrium assumption, data are examined and studies are reworked until the conflict disappears. But the possibility that the model of competitive markets in long-run equilibrium could be inadequate to explain phenomena is not admitted.

[101] Bork, *Antitrust Paradox*, 127.

[102] Posner, *Economic Analysis of Law*, 10.

ATTORNEY: And you maintain that the only way in which this willingness to pay can be determined with certainty is by observing actual transactions voluntarily consummated in the marketplace.

EXPERT: Yes.

ATTORNEY: And where resources are shifted from use to use in accordance with such "voluntary" transactions, you are reasonably confident that the shift reflects a net increase in allocative efficiency.[103]

EXPERT: Yes.

ATTORNEY: In short, as long as individuals and corporations are free to do as they please, private interests and public welfare will be harmonized. Society's resources will be used in the best possible way. Obedience to laissez-faire will help make this the best of all possible worlds.

EXPERT: Yes, but with the qualifications I have noted in my testimony.

ATTORNEY: Namely, that cartels and monopolies are objectionable because they restrict output and raise price, and therefore distort allocative efficiency and diminish consumer welfare.

EXPERT: That is correct.

ATTORNEY: And yet you believe that monopolies—and cartels as well—are subject to erosion by the entry of new competitors.

EXPERT: Yes.

ATTORNEY: As you see it, entry is a ubiquitous threat and even monopoly markets are contestable?

EXPERT: Yes.

ATTORNEY: And there are no barriers to entry?

[103] Ibid., 11.

EXPERT: Correct, except for barriers imposed by government or in the very unlikely event of predation.

ATTORNEY: And, if monopoly nevertheless persists or an industry remains highly concentrated over long periods of time, this is nothing more than evidence of economies of scale and superior efficiency?

EXPERT: Yes.

ATTORNEY: And this superior efficiency is not susceptible to quantitative measurement?

EXPERT: That's right.

JUDGE: [*To the witness*] And we therefore have to take claims of efficiency on faith?

EXPERT: No, Your Honor, not on faith. On the basis of the theory and on the basis of common sense.

ATTORNEY: Isn't your exclusive reliance on price theory to understand economic behavior—indeed, all human behavior—like trying to get from New York to Los Angeles with a road map that stops in Cheyenne, Wyoming?

EXPERT: I don't think so.

ATTORNEY: You know, of course, that many economists would disagree with you. Most would endorse Buchanan's observation that "learning more about how markets work means learning more about how markets work."[104]

JUDGE: Counselor, I am afraid I have reached the limit of my absorptive capacity for the finer points of the dismal science. Would this be a convenient point for a recess?

ATTORNEY: Of course, Your Honor.

JUDGE: Good. We stand adjourned until nine o'clock tomorrow morning.

[104] Buchanan, *What Should Economists Do?* 36–37.

DAY 2 – THE EXAMINATION TURNS TO HORIZONTAL AND VERTICAL MERGERS

The Testimony on Horizontal Mergers and Horizontal Integration

JUDGE: You may resume your examination of the expert.

ATTORNEY: Thank you, Your Honor. [*To the witness*] Section 7 of the Clayton Act, as amended by the Celler-Kefauver Act, prohibits acquisitions where in any line of commerce in any section of the country the effect "may be to substantially lessen competition or tend to create a monopoly."

EXPERT: Yes.

ATTORNEY: In enacting this provision, Congress was concerned with what it considered "the rising tide of concentration" . . .

EXPERT: This is the standard, *Mark I*, all-weather antitrust hobgoblin.[105]

ATTORNEY: [*Continuing*] and wanted to arrest that trend to a lessening of competition in its incipiency—to nip it in the bud.

EXPERT: The difficulty with stopping a trend toward concentration at an early stage is that, as Robert

---

[105] Bork, *Antitrust Paradox*, 202. For compilations of evidence to the contrary, see Michael E. Porter, *The Competitive Advantage of Nations* (New York: Free Press, 1990); and Leonard W. Weiss, ed., *Concentration and Price* (Cambridge: MIT Press, 1989).

Bork has made clear, the very existence of the trend indicates that there are emerging efficiencies or economies of scale. These efficiencies may be due to engineering and production developments, new distribution techniques, or new control and management techniques. In any event, the fact that they exist indicates that larger size is more efficient, and hence socially desirable. To stop such concentration trends in an industry on the basis of some misguided incipiency theory would prevent society from realizing the very efficiencies that competition is supposed to encourage.[106]

ATTORNEY: If an industry displays these emerging efficiencies or economies of scale, couldn't they be realized by internal expansion instead of merger?

EXPERT: Yes, but at much higher social cost.

JUDGE: [*To the witness*] I must remind you that your position is directly at odds with established precedent. According to the Supreme Court, "[I]nternal expansion is more likely to be the result of increased demand for the company's products and is more likely to provide increased investment in plants, more jobs and greater output. Conversely, expansion through merger is more likely to reduce available consumer choice while providing no increase in industry capacity, jobs or output."[107]

EXPERT: I understand that, Your Honor, but merger is a quicker and hence more cost-effective way to capture emerging economies of scale. In any event, the decision to merge or to expand internally should be

---

[106] Bork, *Antitrust Paradox*, , 205–6.
[107] Brown Shoe Co. v. United States, 370 U.S. 294 (1962).

left to the firms involved. If the law artificially
blocks mergers, it may force a firm to adopt the more
expensive internal expansion strategy. It makes it
more difficult and more costly to achieve the increased efficiencies that firms anticipate from larger
size. This forces higher costs not only on the firm
but on society at large.[108]

ATTORNEY: [*Resuming the examination*] Are you saying that the primary motive for mergers is to capture
existing or emerging economies of scale?

EXPERT: There are multiple motivations for mergers.
Mergers enable firms to exploit economies of scale
sooner than they could by internal expansion. Mergers are instrumental in placing assets in the hands of
superior managers. Also, where mergers occur pur-
suant to a takeover bid, they are one way of punish-
ing inefficient or corrupt managers.[109] If improved efficiency were not the purpose of mergers, mergers
would not take place. The fact that they do indicates
that this is indeed the purpose that rational firms
have in mind when consummating mergers.

ATTORNEY: You refer to rational firms making rational
decisions that will promote efficiency. But don't we
have to distinguish who, precisely, these decisionmakers are, what their interests are, and whether
their interests are, in fact, congruent with corporate
efficiency? For example, T. Boone Pickens, the quint-
essential raider of the 1980s, argues that there is a
separation in corporate America between those who
own the corporation, the stockholders, and the man-

---

[108] Bork, *Antitrust Paradox*, 207.
[109] Posner, *Antitrust Law*, 96.

agement that controls the corporation. He claims that CEOs typically own a small share of a firm's stock, yet have discretionary control over billions of dollars of the firm's assets. As a result, Pickens claims, corporate managers behave like bureaucrats, pursuing goals that benefit them personally, but at the expense of the organization's efficiency—including expansion of their corporate empires through mergers and acquisitions that cannot be justified on the grounds of economic efficiency.[110]

EXPERT: Economic theory suggests that corporate managers may indeed have incentives to expand their firms beyond the size that maximizes shareholder wealth. But this tendency is limited by competition in product and factor markets, which tends to drive prices toward minimum average cost in an activity.[111]

ATTORNEY: Whatever the purpose behind particular mergers, can we really be certain that the effect will be a predictable enhancement of efficiency?

EXPERT: Not necessarily. But there is no need for concern. The market will ensure that efficiency-enhancing mergers will survive and that unsuccessful mergers will be voluntarily undone.

---

[110] T. Boone Pickens, *Boone* (Boston: Houghton Mifflin Co., 1987), 280–90. For the original statement of this thesis, and a thorough exploration of its implications and consequences, see Adolph Berle and Gardner Means, *The Modern Corporation and Private Property* (New York: Macmillan, 1937).
[111] Michael C. Jensen, "The Takeover Controversy: Analysis and Evidence," in John C. Coffee, Louis Lowenstein, and Susan Rose-Ackerman, eds., *Knights, Raiders and Targets* (New York: Oxford University Press, 1988), 321–22.

ATTORNEY: But doesn't this involve a social cost? Doesn't a perpetual merging/unmerging, acquisition/divestiture process represent a substantial opportunity cost in terms of misplaced managerial energies—an unproductive and even counterproductive investment of time, money, and resources?

EXPERT: Perhaps. But that is the way a free market works. It is still less costly than prolonged antitrust litigation and dubious court opinions, which ignore basic economic principles. Economic welfare is significantly served by maintaining a good market for capital assets.[112]

ATTORNEY: Let's concentrate on the real world for a moment and examine the relation between merger-induced firm size and efficiency. Take, for example, the American steel industry, which is an oligopoly dominated by horizontally and vertically integrated giants. Virtually every one of these companies started—and subsequently grew—not by building facilities but by buying them. Often the individual parts didn't add up to an organic whole. The result was an amalgam of helter-skelter consolidations devoid of operating efficiency.[113]

---

[112] Donald Turner, "Conglomerate Mergers and Section 7 of the Clayton Act," *Harvard Law Review* 78 (1965): 1317.

[113] In the 1930s, for example, Ford, Bacon & Davis, a management consulting firm retained by U.S. Steel to conduct an internal efficiency study, found that the nation's largest steelmaker was "a big, sprawling, inert giant, whose production operations were improperly coordinated; suffering from a lack of a long-run planning agency; relying on an antiquated system of cost accounting; with an inadequate knowledge of the costs or the relative profitability of the many thousands of items it sold; with production and cost standards generally below those considered every-day practice in other industries; with inadequate knowledge of its domestic markets and

EXPERT: That's just anecdotal and episodic evidence.

ATTORNEY: Isn't it also a fact that the record of the giant integrated steel companies is most notable for its technological backwardness and lethargic innovation? Didn't the American steel oligopoly lag significantly—vis-à-vis both its smaller domestic rivals and its foreign competitors—in adopting such major technological breakthroughs in basic steelmaking as the oxygen furnace and continuous casting?

EXPERT: And the oligopoly paid the price for it. It lost market share to the minimills and to imports. The free market worked. It punished lackluster performance.

ATTORNEY: But how long did it take the market to punish deficient performance? Three decades?

EXPERT: Approximately.

ATTORNEY: And weren't there enormous economic and social costs involved, as more than four hundred thousand jobs were lost in steel between 1955 and 1987, with devastating impact on towns, cities, and communities?[114]

EXPERT: Yes, indeed. The market is a stern taskmaster.

---

no clear appreciation of its opportunities in foreign markets; with less efficient production facilities than its rivals had . . . ." U.S. Congress, *Hearings on the Study of Monopoly Power*, 81st Cong., 1st sess., 1950, pt. 4-A, 967. And today, eight decades after its founding, and after considerable shrinkage in its relative size, U.S. Steel is still "one of America's most hierarchial, bureaucratic managements . . . an inbred, centralized, autocratic bureaucracy that stifles change." William C. Symonds, "The Toughest Job in Business," *Business Week*, Feb. 25, 1985, 50–51. In financial circles, neither the corporation nor most of the other steel giants are perceived as paragons of efficiency.

[114] U.S. General Accounting Office, *International Trade: The Health of the U.S. Steel Industry*, Report no. GAO/NSIAD-89-193 (July 1989).

ATTORNEY: What would have happened if the mergers that created the steel oligopoly had been blocked in their incipiency? Wouldn't we have had a more competitive and more efficient American steel industry today—an industry that could stand on its own feet without government protection, and which might have escaped these economic and social disasters?

EXPERT: Your point is entirely speculative and conjectural. I am satisfied that in the case of steel, the magic of the market worked precisely in accordance with what economic theory would predict.

ATTORNEY: What about automobiles? What do you make of the statement by Elliott M. Estes, a former president of General Motors, who believes that "Chevrolet is such a big monster that you twist its tail and nothing happens at the other end for months and months. It is so gigantic that there isn't any way to really run it. You just try to keep track of it"? And why did General Motors have to create Saturn as a freestanding subsidiary to operate as independently as possible from its bureaucratic parent? Might there not be substantial efficiency gains if other major divisions of GM were similarly freed from the burdens of corporate giantism?

EXPERT: Again, you are indulging in speculation and conjecture.

ATTORNEY: And what about the mounting evidence that mergers don't work well, not only in economic treatises but also in articles in respected business journals—"Small Is Beautiful Now in Manufacturing"; "Do Mergers Really Work? Not Very Often, and That Raises Even More Questions about the

Current Merger Mania"; "Splitting Up, It's the Opposite of Merger Mania: Companies Divesting Assets, Spinning off Divisions, Even Liquidating Themselves"; "Big Won't Work"; "Big Goes Bust"? Such evidence doesn't seem to comport with the theory you have articulated.

EXPERT: Journalists are sheep. As I have said before, if a given merger is viable, it will survive. If not, it will eventually be undone. Let the market decide. Don't interfere with the market process. Keep the government off the backs of business.

JUDGE: Hold on a moment! [*To the witness*] Are you saying that all government intervention is undesirable? Are you saying that section 7 of the Clayton Act should be ignored altogether? Are you suggesting that I and other judges ignore the original will of Congress and that, instead, we engage in judicial legislation? Surely you're aware that in passing the Celler-Kefauver Act of 1950, Congress made its purpose clear—"to limit further increases in the level of economic concentration resulting from corporate mergers and acquisitions"?[115]

EXPERT: With all due respect Your Honor, I prefer the approach suggested by Judge Bork and Judge Posner that, in principle, mergers resulting in market control of up to 60 or 70 percent should not be challenged. They should automatically be considered lawful.[116]

ATTORNEY: [*Resuming the examination*] I am surprised to hear you say that. Surely, you must be aware that

---

[115] S. Rept. 1775, 81st Cong., 2d sess., 1950, 3.
[116] Bork, *Antitrust Paradox*, 221.

the Bork/Posner position is at substantial variance
with that of George Stigler—a Chicago school stal-
wart and a Nobel laureate in economics. You must
recall that according to Stigler, every merger by a
firm with 20 percent or more of an industry's output
should automatically be presumed to have violated
the Clayton Act (as amended by the Celler-Kefauver
Act). Such stringent action, Stigler wrote, "deserves
a place of high priority in the antitrust policy of the
United States."[117] It would preserve competition
without undercutting good economic performance.

EXPERT: That may have been Stigler's position some
thirty or thirty-five years ago. I doubt whether it is
his position today.

ATTORNEY: Nevertheless, isn't it a fact that the Bork/
Posner standard would impose Sherman Act—that
is, monopoly—standards on adjudication of the antimerger law?

EXPERT: Judge Bork is not as inflexible as you imply. He
has indicated a willingness to compromise the 60 to
70 percent standard. One of his suggestions is to
make presumptively lawful all horizontal mergers
up to the point where an industry would be left with
at least three significant companies.[118]

ATTORNEY: In practice, what would the application of
such a standard imply?

EXPERT: In a fragmented market, the maximum market
share a firm would be permitted to attain by merger
would be set at 40 percent. In a market, where one

[117] George Stigler, "Mergers and Preventive Antitrust Policy," *University
of Pennsylvania Law Review* 104 (1955): 181–82, 184.
[118] Bork, *Antitrust Paradox*, 221–22.

company already had 50 percent, it could not con-
summate any additional mergers, and no other company could use mergers to achieve a market share
above 30 percent—except under extraordinary circumstances, such as the imminent failure of one of
the merger partners.[119]

ATTORNEY: Are you saying that by the Bork standard, a
merger between U.S. Steel and Bethlehem Steel, the
No. 1 and No. 2 companies in the industry, would be
permissible? Or a merger between Ford and Chrysler,
the No. 2 and No. 3 companies in the auto industry?
Wouldn't such mergers cement existing oligopolies
and thus tend substantially to lessen competition
within the meaning of section 7?

EXPERT: No, because there is little likelihood that the
resulting firms could successfully restrict output and
thus detract from consumer welfare.

ATTORNEY: Why not?

EXPERT: In large part, because of the ubiquity of potential competition and the fear of entry by competitors.
It would not be rational behavior for the merged
firms to attempt a restriction of output and an increase in price.

ATTORNEY: Would you elaborate, please.

The Testimony on Defining the
Relevant Market

EXPERT: The existence of market power and its adverse
consequences for the public have been vastly exag-

[119] Ibid., 222.

gerated because of erroneous definitions of the relevant market.

ATTORNEY: Please explain.

EXPERT: A relevant market definition has both a product component and a geographical component. For example, a firm may seem to have a large market share in the production of cellophane. But there are plentiful substitutes for cellophane, such as glassine paper, wax paper, aluminum foil, film, etc. The cellophane firm must therefore be mindful of the cross-elasticity of demand between its own product and these substitutes. Under the circumstances, it would be irrational for the firm to attempt to restrict output or raise price.

ATTORNEY: Are you saying that in evaluating a particular merger, the relevant product market must be defined so broadly as to include all possible substitutes?

EXPERT: Precisely.

ATTORNEY: And that such a market definition would substantially reduce the nominal concentration ratio of the industry in which a merger is contemplated?

EXPERT: Yes.

ATTORNEY: And that this, in turn, would make the impact of even a sizable merger much less anticompetitive than might appear at first blush?

EXPERT: That is correct.

ATTORNEY: What about the geographical component of the relevant market definition?

EXPERT: Let's take the automobile industry as a concrete example. Suppose we are trying to compute the market share involved in a proposed merger between Ford and Chrysler. A correct definition of the relevant geographical market would have to include not only the domestic producers—that is, the U.S. companies plus the Japanese transplants—but also the sales of foreign producers in the U.S. market. The reason is obvious: The foreign producers have proved their ability to sell in our domestic market and could increase their sales there if the local price were to go up. They could do so simply by diverting sales from their other markets.[120]

ATTORNEY: Is this what you might call supply elasticity?

EXPERT: Precisely. However, two further steps are necessary in arriving at a correct definition of the geographical market. In computing the share of foreign sellers in the U.S. market, we have to include not only their actual sales there, but their potential sales in the United States as well. In other words we have to include the entire output of the foreign producers, regardless of where they may be selling their output at any given moment.[121]

ATTORNEY: And the second step?

EXPERT: The logic of including the total output of foreign producers in the U.S. market also implies the inclusion of their total production capacity, wherever it may be located.[122]

ATTORNEY: Why?

EXPERT: Unused capacity implies that supply is highly elastic. Such capacity can be brought into production

120 William M. Landes and Richard A. Posner, "Market Power in Antitrust Cases," *Harvard Law Review* 94 (Mar. 1981): 963. For a contrary view, see Timothy J. Brennan, "Mistaken Elasticities and Misleading Rules," *Harvard Law Review* 95 (1982): 1849.

121 Landes and Posner, "Market Power in Antitrust Cases," 964.

122 Ibid., 966.

promptly and with no increase in fixed costs. Therefore, it is an effective constraint on the domestic
U.S. producers whenever they may be tempted to restrict output or raise prices and thus do damage to
consumer welfare.

ATTORNEY: In sum, are you saying that in assessing a
merger between leading manufacturers of breakfast
cereals, the relevant *product* market might have to
include egg breeders, croissant bakers, Egg Mac-
Muffin vendors, lox and cream cheese purveyors,
etc.?[123]

EXPERT: Yes, if there is found to be a sufficient cross-
elasticity of demand between these products and
breakfast cereals.

ATTORNEY: Are you saying that in assessing a merger
between leading producers of laptop computers, the
relevant *geographical* market would include the entire world?

EXPERT: Yes, if there is a high cross-elasticity of supply
among actual and potential makers of such computers.

ATTORNEY: If you compute concentration ratios and
market shares by that method, and if you apply the
Bork/Posner standard to judging the legality of horizontal mergers, can you think of *any* merger that
would fail to pass muster?

EXPERT: Conceivably. But horizontal mergers, because
of their beneficial effect on efficiency and hence
their contribution to consumer welfare, should be
condemned only if they have the power to restrict

---

[123] Michael Pertschuk, "Love That Market," *The New Republic*, May 14,
1984, 11.

output and raise prices. Few mergers have that potential.

ATTORNEY: Well, your theory may lead you to believe that. But, as we say in west Texas, that's not the way the cow eats the cabbage.

EXPERT: We'll just have to agree to disagree.

The Testimony on Whether Globalization of Markets Has Made Antitrust an Anachronism

ATTORNEY: Very well. However, since you've just discussed what you consider to be the global aspect of the geographic relevant market, I'd like to ask your opinion of how the so-called internationalization of markets affects the relevance of domestic antitrust policy generally?

EXPERT: It has rendered it more obsolete than ever.

ATTORNEY: Why is that?

EXPERT: Because effective foreign competition serves as a more expedient and efficient check on competitive abuses by domestic firms than U.S. antitrust enforcers can ever hope to be.[124] For example, even though the domestic automobile industry is composed of only a few firms, who would seriously accuse it of monopolizing its markets in the light of fierce international competition?[125] Even if GM and Ford were to merge together, the combined firm would still

---

[124] Interview with Charles F. Rule, Assistant Attorney General, Antitrust Division, Department of Justice, *Antitrust Law Journal* 58 (1989): 377, 382.
[125] DiLorenzo, "The Rhetoric of Antitrust," 3.

face competition from Japanese, German, Korean, French, and British producers.

ATTORNEY: But aren't you failing to take into account the fact that domestic firms can neutralize foreign competition through joint ventures, global cartels, or mergers with their major foreign rivals? In the automobile industry, for example, you must agree that the advent of foreign competition seriously shook the domestic oligopoly from its decades-long, postwar somnolence?

EXPERT: Yes, competition in the U.S. market for cars and steel increased when Japanese and other foreign companies became important players.[126]

ATTORNEY: But isn't such competition now undermined by the "joint ventures" that have been proliferated in recent years between the U.S. auto oligopoly and its major rivals abroad—joint ventures that now include GM-Toyota, GM-Isuzu, GM-Suzuki, GM-Daewoo, GM-Saab, Ford-Mazda, Ford-Mazda-Kia, Ford-VW, Ford-Nissan, Chrysler-Mitsubishi, Chrysler-Samsung, Chrysler-VW, and Chrysler-Peugeot, among others.[127] These, in turn, are embedded in an even more expansive network of joint ventures, involving the world's leading auto firms. To quote the London *Economist*, "What's the connection between Porsche and Suzuki? Well, Volkswagen's Audi division assembles some Porsches; VW has a Brazilian carmaking joint venture with Ford; Ford is work-

---

[126] Gary S. Becker, "Antitrust's Only Proper Quarry: Collusion," *Business Week*, Oct. 12, 1987, 22.

[127] Walter Adams and James Brock, "Joint Ventures, Antitrust, and Transnational Cartelization," *Northwestern Journal of International Law and Business* 11 (1991): 433–83.

ing with Nissan to develop a new American mini-van; Nissan owns 5% of Fuji Heavy Industries (which makes Subaru cars); Subaru has a joint-venture car plant in America with Isuzu; General Motors owns 38% of Isuzu—and GM owns 5% of Suzuki."[128] Now, Professor, I ask you, doesn't an expansive web of joint ventures of this breadth and intricacy transform the relationship between these firms from one of competitors to one of global partners?

EXPERT: Not necessarily. As President Reagan's Federal Trade Commission chairman, James C. Miller, ruled in the case of the GM-Toyota joint venture, transnational joint ventures can provide valuable opportunities for American auto firms to learn more efficient manufacturing techniques and thus make them more competitive with foreign producers.[129]

ATTORNEY: But aside from the implication that GM's size has failed to promote efficiency, is it really the case that competition is enhanced when transnational joint ventures turn the participants into intimate partners? If we take airlines as another example, mergers have concentrated the U.S. airline industry into the hands of a few mega-carriers, who

---

[128] "Spot the Difference," The Economist, Feb. 24, 1990, 74. Similarly, joint ventures in steel now include U.S. Steel Corp.–Kobe Steel, LTV–Sumitomo Steel, Armco–Itoh Steel, Armco–Kawasaki Steel, National Steel–Nippon Kokan Steel, Inland Steel-Nippon Steel, and Wheeling Pittsburgh-Nisshan Steel. See Adams and Brock, "Joint Ventures, Antitrust, and Transnational Cartelization."

[129] Statement of James C. Miller, Chairman, Federal Trade Commission, concerning GM/Toyota joint venture, Apr. 11, 1984, reprinted in U.S. Congress, House, Subcommittee on Commerce, Transportation, and Tourism, Future of the Automobile Industry, 98th Cong., 2d sess., 1984, 495–96.

have constructed hub monopolies at major airports and cities across the country. Now, the U.S. oligopoly is rapidly linking up with major foreign air carriers—their major remaining source of potential competition—through a host of joint ventures and joint operating agreements: United Airlines–British Air, United Airlines–Alitalia, Northwest-KLM, Scandanavian Airlines System (SAS)–Eastern/ Continental, Delta-Swissair, and USAir–Air France.[130] Don't joint ventures between firms of this size and stature undermine the efficacy of global competition as a substitute for domestic antitrust policy?

EXPERT: Not at all. Globalization of markets means that whether they are partners or not, even firms in industries previously thought to suffer from "the oligopoly problem" face competitive challenges from a worldwide set of enterprises[131]—competition that, as former FTC chairman James C. Miller has pointed out, joint ventures typically enhance.

ATTORNEY: But, again, do they really face effective rivalry if, as in the case of the petroleum industry, the world's largest firms are intertwined and interlinked with one another at virtually every turn—both at home and abroad—through joint exploration, joint bidding, joint production, and joint pipeline agreements?[132] In jointly constructing and operating pipelines, for example, don't the major oil companies

[130] Adams and Brock, "Joint Ventures, Antitrust, and Transnational Cartelization."

[131] William F. Baxter, "The Common Core of Antitrust Concern," in *Antitrust in the Competitive World of the 1980s*, Conference Board Research Bulletin no. 112, (New York: Conference Board, 1982).

[132] See Walter Adams and James W. Brock, "The 'New Learning' and the Euthanasia of Antitrust," *California Law Review* 74 (1986): 1515, 1529–32.

effectively allocate market shares among themselves in the course of allocating pipeline shipments? Aren't they forced to reveal to one another their long-term plans for expansion, for contraction, and for sales and marketing—and to do so in intricate detail? And doesn't this militate against effective competition between them?

EXPERT: To return to the hypothetical, if you had a merger between Ford and Chrysler, you would have not only General Motors but a whole raft of Japanese, German, Korean, and British competitors, who would eat them alive if they tried to raise their prices above the competitive level. For that reason, there is simply nothing to worry about in a merger of that sort.[133]

ATTORNEY: But is it realistic to hypothesize that these firms will, in your words, "eat each other alive," if they are partners? Aren't you ignoring not only the existence of transnational joint ventures but also the extensively documented history of global cartels, encompassing domestic and foreign producers, which flourished during the earlier era of radical laissez-faire between the two world wars?[134] Moreover, aren't you also failing to consider the possibility that if, say, GM and Ford were to merge together, the merged firm would be capable of exercising substantial political clout in obtaining government import restraints limiting foreign competition—govern-

[133] Robert Bork, *Antitrust Issues for A New Administration*, Conference Board Research Bulletin no. 233 (New York: Conference Board, 1989), 20.
[134] See Adams and Brock, "The 'New Learning,' " 1522–27, and the extensive sources cited therein.

ment restraints such as the quotas imposed on Japanese imports in the American market during the 1980s at the behest of the Big Three auto firms?

EXPERT: It is my professional opinion that as long as government refrains from intervening, the stiffest challenge to a domestic conspiracy will come from foreign producers.[135]

The Testimony on Vertical Mergers and Vertical Integration

ATTORNEY: Turning now to vertical integration and vertical mergers, you are, of course, familiar with these concepts?

EXPERT: Yes. A firm is said to be vertically integrated if it operates at more than one stage of a series of stages within the same industry, ranging from raw materials to intermediate processing to final distribution to consumers. A vertical merger is a merger between firms operating at two or more of these successive stages within the same industry.

ATTORNEY: In other words, a vertical merger would describe a merger between an oil and refining firm and, say, a petroleum pipeline operator and a retail gasoline station. A movie production company's acquisition of local theaters would provide another example. Wouldn't the result in either case be the creation of a vertically integrated firm operating at two or more major stages within the same industry?

[135] Becker, "Antitrust's Only Proper Quarry," 22.

EXPERT: That is correct. But I hasten to stress that vertical integration is ubiquitous.[136]

ATTORNEY: But is it not true that some industries are characterized by an especially pronounced vertical structure? In the petroleum industry, for example, there are two distinct groups of firms. On the one hand, there are thousands of smaller, nonintegrated firms, operating at only one stage of the industry. On the other hand, there is a handful of vertically integrated giants, such as Exxon and Mobil, which simultaneously operate at each of the industry's major stages of production, refining, transportation, and retailing.

EXPERT: Every firm in the economy is vertically integrated in the sense that goods and services are transmitted within it and not offered on any market.[137] For example, you assume that a refinery is an indecomposable technological unit. But your assumption is incorrect.[138]

ATTORNEY: Why is that?

EXPERT: Even within the single stage of the petroleum refinery, numerous separable operations can be identified: How should the storage tanks for intermediate and finished product be owned and operated? Should the quality control laboratory be independently owned and operated?[139] Vertical integration is ubiquitous, therefore, because the production pro-

[136] John S. McGee, *Industrial Organization* (Englewood Cliffs, NJ: Prentice Hall, 1988), 272–73.

[137] Bork, *Antitrust Paradox*, 226.

[138] Oliver E. Williamson, *The Economic Institutions of Capitalism* (New York: Free Press, 1985), 106.

[139] Ibid.

cesses in which any firm is engaged are further divisible and, in principle, could be undertaken by separate firms. Many people overlook this.[140]

ATTORNEY: But as an advocate for the market system, how do you explain the existence of vertical integration? After all, is it not true that a vertical merger between firms that formerly interacted as buyer and seller across a market removes their transactions from the market? As a result, don't vertical mergers reduce the range of economic activity subject to the market?

EXPERT: Vertical integration is merely an instance of replacing a market transaction with administrative direction because the latter is believed to be a more efficient method of coordination.[141] Maintaining or increasing the number of markets artificially would be an expensive mistake.[142]

ATTORNEY: Is it your opinion, then, that vertical mergers and vertical integration displace markets because markets are inefficient?

EXPERT: Buying and selling in external markets cost resources. There are costs of searching out buyers and sellers, transacting, contracting, enforcing, and so on.[143]

ATTORNEY: I want to make sure I understand your position. So, again, is it your opinion that vertical integration arises because the market system is flawed?

[140] McGee, *Industrial Organization*, 272–73.
[141] Bork, *Antitrust Paradox*, 227.
[142] McGee, *Industrial Organization*, 276.
[143] Ibid., 272.

EXPERT: In the context of general equilibrium theory, the contours of the business firm are dictated largely by the need to overcome market imperfections. Contracts that deal with all future contingencies cannot practicably be written; in the absence of such contracts, individuals do behave opportunistically; gains from developing information are difficult to appropriate; and the transaction costs of dealing entirely through spot markets are often prohibitively high. Thus, firms are motivated by the need to overcome market imperfections.[144]

ATTORNEY: Would you explain why centralized hierarchial control is superior to the market as an instrument for organizing a society's economic work?

EXPERT: Certainly. An authoritative order is a more efficient way to settle conflicts than haggling or litigation. Conflicts between independent firms can be settled by fiat only rarely, if at all. Internal organization, having access to a more finely graded status system than the market, thus enjoys a communication advantage, in relation to the market, in the degree to which the needs for authenticity, authoritativeness, and intelligibility are especially great. Moreover, the compliance instruments that the firm can bring to bear on its employees to promote favored and discourage unfavored outcomes are more refined and selective.[145]

ATTORNEY: But isn't it a fact that General Motors is highly vertically integrated, producing more than 70

[144] William F. Baxter, "The Viability of Vertical Restraints Doctrine," *California Law Review* 75 (1987): 933, 948.

[145] Oliver E. Williamson, *Markets and Hierarchies* (New York: Free Press, 1975), 101, 102, 104.

percent of the parts and components for its cars, and yet considerable empirical evidence suggests that such vertical integration undermines the firm's efficiency, in important part by impairing GM's flexibility?[146] And isn't it also a fact that prior to the breakup of the Bell system's vertically integrated monopoly, the firm's own officials admitted patronizing their internal supply divisions despite the fact that outside equipment suppliers had surpassed them in technological innovativeness and efficiency of production?[147] Now, in the light of such evidence,

---

[146] Noting that General Motors suffers the highest unit costs in the industry, *Business Week* has reported that GM's "integrated factories, which make more than two-thirds of the parts used in GM cars, have become a high-cost problem." William J. Hampton and James R. Norman, "GM: What Went Wrong," *Business Week*, Mar. 16, 1987, 103. The conservative London *Economist* has observed: "Mastery of a business requires a constant search for ways to bring new technologies and techniques into it. But usually it is better to hire new skills, and to buy innovative components, than to acquire the companies that provide them. The technology of the motor car and its manufacture is evolving so fast that the sensible carmaker keeps its options open. The security and exclusivity of the 'tied supplier' often prove a trap." *The Economist*, Dec. 13, 1986, 15. See also Doron Levin, "Groping Giant: In a High-Tech Drive, GM Falls below Rivals in Auto Profit Margins," *Wall Street Journal*, July 22, 1986, 14, reporting that GM managers feel obligated to procure parts in house, which undermines the efficiency of the firm's parts production units.

Similarly, in steel it is the non–vertically integrated, specialized "mini-mill" firms that are the efficiency and innovation leaders in the industry, and these firms have won market share not only from the vertically integrated American steel giants but from foreign producers as well. See Walter Adams and James W. Brock, *The Bigness Complex* (New York: Pantheon, 1987), 34–38, 57–59.

[147] The following confidential statements were made by AT & T officials, evaluating the firm's performance as a vertically integrated monopolist: "I want to comment on our progress in integrated circuits. I have been concerned with the long time needed to design and get models made of a new device, the distressingly low yield in manufacture and resulting high cost of many devices that had reached the stage of [Western Electric, AT & T's vertically integrated equipment production division] manufac-

how can you maintain that internal hierarchial control is economically superior to the market?

EXPERT: Because vertical integration economizes on
transactions by harmonizing interests and permit-
ting a wider variety of sensitive incentive and control processes to be activated.[148]

ATTORNEY: So as an advocate for the market system, is
it your opinion that the choice between the market
system, on the one hand, and a system of administra-
tive-hierarchial control of economic activity, on the
other hand, depends merely upon the relative efficiency of each?

---

ture, and the general unhappiness in our system development areas, *espe-*
cially as people in those areas observed the wide and growing range of
devices that seemed to be available from outside suppliers . . . ." "[E]ven
as late as 1959, more than ten years after the invention, the rate of manufacture of transistors at [AT & T's Allentown facility] was only one to two
hundred thousand units a year. *On the outside, however, the rate had*
reached a level of several tens of millions per year." "Even though most of
the basic discoveries in the field were made at Bell Telephone Laboratories,
until recently the Bell System was behind outside competition in the production of integrated circuit devices." "During the last several years, it has
become increasingly apparent that we have sadly neglected PBX development. . . . There are many kinds of PBX's appearing in the U.S. . . . There
is no doubt that we have a rough road ahead." Quoted in U.S. Congress,
House, *The Communications Act of 1978: Hearings before the Subcom-*
mittee on Communications of the Committee on Interstate and Foreign
Commerce, 95th Cong., 2d sess., 1979, vol. 2, pt. 1, 817, 833 (emphasis
added).

In United States v. American Tel. & Tel. Co., 524 F. Supp. 1336 (D.D.C.
1981), Judge Greene found numerous "examples of independent business
or engineering judgments by the [local Bell operating companies] to buy
from the general trade because of lower cost, better quality, or desirable
features. Presumably in these cases the Operating Companies considered
that the advantages of the general trade products (or the inadequacies of
the [AT & T–owned Western Electric equipment manufacturing subsid-
iary] offerings) outweighed the efficiencies to be gained from vertical integration. But they were, nonetheless, persuaded to change their minds and
to purchase from Western instead—even if that meant waiting for an as yet
nonexistent Western product to come on the market." Ibid., 1373 n.157.

[148] Williamson, *Markets and Hierarchies,* 104.

EXPERT: In deciding between alternative methods for organizing transactions, the key question is which has the superior efficiency properties. Once we adopt this orientation, internal corporate organization is seen less as a consequence of technology and more as the result of a comparative assessment of markets and hierarchies.[149]

ATTORNEY: As an economic scientist, how would you ascertain if a trend toward vertical integration was truly efficient in fact, as opposed to theory?

EXPERT: From a strictly scientific point of view, it must be efficient.

ATTORNEY: Why is that?

EXPERT: Because it occurs. When the efficiencies obtainable through vertical integration become apparent, a trend toward vertical integration will develop. Such trends are merely the responses of business people to changing circumstances. What is incipient in any such trend is the attainment of new efficiency.[150]

ATTORNEY: As a scientific matter, is it possible to observe and measure these efficiencies you are describing?

EXPERT: These cost savings are difficult either to demonstrate or to measure.[151] They must be assumed on the basis of observed behavior.

ATTORNEY: Assumptions don't feed the bulldog. But let's turn now to some anticompetitive consequences that may grow out of vertical relationships.

EXPERT: There are none.

[149] Ibid., 88. For a perspective on the vertical integration debate, see Rudolph J. Peritz, "A Genealogy of Vertical Restraints Doctrine," *Hastings Law Journal* 40 (1989): 511–76.

[150] Bork, *Antitrust Paradox*, 227, 234.

[151] McGee, *Industrial Organization*, 281.

ATTORNEY: I beg your pardon?

EXPERT: Vertical relationships are never anticompetitive.[152] The fact that two firms stand in a relationship of potential supplier and potential customer is not in and of itself troublesome.[153]

JUDGE: Excuse me, but I am constrained to remind the witness that this answer flies in the face of a long series of Supreme Court precedents—the Yellow Cab case of 1947,[154] the Paramount Pictures case of 1948,[155] the Du Pont–GM case of 1957,[156] the Brown Shoe Company case of 1962,[157] and the Ford-Autolite case of 1972.[158] Given these precedents, are you still arguing that the concept of vertical market power is an optical illusion—that anticompetitive behavior is exclusively a horizontal problem?

EXPERT: Again, with due deference, Your Honor, I would have to say that that is my view.

ATTORNEY: [*Resuming the examination*] Let me pursue that point. Take resale price maintenance for example. If retail dealers selling mousetraps conspired to charge the same price, you would consider this to be an anticompetitive cartel harmful to consumer welfare and destructive of economic efficiency, would you not?

EXPERT: Of course.

[152] Interview with Assistant Attorney General William F. Baxter, *U.S. News & World Report*, Aug. 3, 1981, 51.

[153] "Big Shift in Antitrust Policy: Interview with William Baxter, Assistant Attorney General for Antitrust," *Dun's Review*, August 1981, 40.

[154] United States v. Yellow Cab Co., 332 U.S. 218 (1947).

[155] United States v. Paramount Pictures, Inc., 334 U.S. 131 (1948).

[156] United States v. E. I. Du Pont de Nemours & Co., 353 U.S. 586 (1957).

[157] Brown Shoe Co. v. United States, 370 U.S. 294 (1962).

[158] Ford Motor Co. v. United States, 405 U.S. 562 (1972).

ATTORNEY: But if through resale price maintenance agreements, a producer of mousetraps were to require *all* its retailers to sell the product at identical prices, would this vertically imposed kind of price fixing not be just as anticompetitive? Would it not be just as harmful to consumer welfare as horizontal conspiracy among competing retailers?

EXPERT: Not at all. As Attorney General William Baxter has shown, in theory such vertical resale price maintenance agreements can promote consumer welfare and economic efficiency: By fixing retail prices, manufacturers can induce dealers to compete by providing a variety of other services for their customers, including local advertising, various point-of-purchase services, well-trained salespeople, and the like. For these reasons, vertical resale price maintenance is typically procompetitive.[159]

ATTORNEY: But are you aware that in 1952, seventeen economists at the University of Chicago—including Nobel laureate Milton Friedman—argued just the opposite? To quote from their letter to the House Antitrust Subcommittee, urging the repeal of "fair trade" laws allowing such agreements: "Resale price maintenance reduces competition in two principal ways: It eliminates price competition among distrib-

[159] Letter from William F. Baxter to Mr. Edward T. Borda, President, Association of General Merchandise Chains, May 24, 1982, reprinted in *Antitrust Law Journal* 52 (1983): 714. See also Mr. Baxter's responses to congressional questions concerning vertical price fixing in U.S. Congress, Senate, Committee on Small Business, *Hearing on Federal Antitrust Enforcement and Small Business*, 97th Cong., 2d sess., 1982, 122–23, 131–34.

Professor (and former FTC Commissioner) Pitofsky points out that where producers desire retailers to provide additional services, they can simply contract with them to do so, without the necessity of vertically fixing prices. Robert Pitofsky, "Why Dr. Miles Was Right," *Regulation*, Jan./Feb. 1984, 29.

utors and retailers and thus has the same effect as horizontal price fixing." Resale price maintenance, they wrote, also "facilitates concerted action between manufacturers not easily detected, and thereby reduces competition at the manufacturing level."[160] And you must also be aware of numerous studies finding that vertical price fixing tends to substantially inflate prices to consumers, in some cases by as much as 40 percent.[161] Indeed, Congressman Jack Brooks, chairman of the House Judiciary Committee, estimates that resale price maintenance costs American consumers twenty billion dollars a year.[162]

---

[160] U.S. Congress, House, Subcommittee on Antitrust, *Hearings on Resale Price Maintenance*, 82d Cong., 2d sess., 1952, 868. For an early condemnation of vertical price fixing by another Chicagoan, see Ward S. Bowman, "Resale Price Maintenance—A Monopoly Problem," *Journal of Business* 25 (July 1952): 141.

Ronald Reagan also criticized the price-inflating impact of vertical price fixing under the "fair trade" laws: If we were to repeal these laws, he argued in 1975, "some prices should begin going down as a result. That may not lick inflation, but it should help." *Congressional Record*, Jan. 23, 1975, 1268.

[161] For surveys and sources, see Walter Adams and James W. Brock, "The Political Economy of Antitrust Exemptions," *Washburn Law Journal* 29 (Winter 1990): 225–26; and F. M. Scherer and David Ross, *Industrial Market Structure and Economic Performance*, 3d ed. (Boston: Houghton Mifflin, 1990), 555–56.

For example, Professor Sharon Oster found that when Levi Strauss was prohibited from engaging in vertical price fixing, the price of Levi jeans fell 40 percent. Oster, "The FTC v. Levi Strauss: An Analysis of the Economic Issues," in Ronald N. Lafferty, Robert H. Lande, and John B. Kirkwood, eds., *Impact Evaluations of Federal Trade Commission Vertical Restraints Cases* (Washington, D.C.: Federal Trade Commission, 1984), 73.

For additional studies of the anticompetitive, price-inflating effects of other kinds of vertical restraints, see Willard F. Mueller, "The Sealy Restraints: Restrictions on Free Riding or Output?" 1989 *Wisconsin Law Review*: 1255, and the testimony of Professor W. John Jordan in U.S. Congress, Senate, Committee on the Judiciary, *Hearings on the Malt Beverage Interbrand Competition Act*, 98th Cong., 1st and 2d sess., 1984, 77–82.

[162] *Wall Street Journal*, Feb. 27, 1991, B4.

EXPERT: As Judge Easterbrook points out, if consumers are dissatisfied, the competitive market, not the courts, can best correct the problem.[163]

ATTORNEY: Leaving aside resale price maintenance, let us come back to the anticompetitive effects that may arise from vertical mergers.

EXPERT: As I have told you before, vertical relationships, including vertical mergers, are never anticompetitive.

ATTORNEY: Would you explain, please.

EXPERT: A merger between Bethlehem Steel and Ford, for instance, would be a vertical merger. The vertical aspects would not trouble me.[164]

ATTORNEY: Why is that?

EXPERT: Because vertical mergers do not create or increase the firm's power to restrict output.[165]

ATTORNEY: Why not?

EXPERT: Because monopoly power depends upon the percentage of the market occupied by the firm. Vertical integration does not increase the percentage of the market controlled by the firm. If a manufacturing firm acquires 50 percent of all distributors, and sells only through them, there is no increase in its power to affect price.[166] Moreover, the theory makes it clear that vertical integration does not affect the firm's pricing and output policies. If, for example, a firm operates at both the manufacturing and retailing levels of an industry, it maximizes overall profit

---

[163] Frank Easterbrook, "Restricted Dealing Is a Way to Compete," *Regulation*, Jan./Feb. 1984, 27.

[164] "Big Shift in Antitrust Policy," 40.

[165] Bork, *Antitrust Paradox*, 231.

[166] Bork, "Vertical Integration and Competitive Processes," in J. Fred Weston and Sam Peltzman, eds., *Public Policy toward Mergers* (Pacific Palisades, Calif.: Goodyear Publishing Co., 1969), 142.

by setting the output at each level as though the units were independent of one another.[167] /

ATTORNEY: Are you familiar with the practice commonly referred to as the vertical price squeeze?

EXPERT: Yes. A manufacturer acquires a retailer and allegedly imposes losses on other retailers by raising wholesale prices, by lowering retail prices, or by doing both simultaneously.[168]

ATTORNEY: Do you consider this to be an anticompetitive problem?

EXPERT: No.

ATTORNEY: Why not?

EXPERT: It is theoretically impossible for a firm to sell products to itself for less than it sells them to outside firms, because the real cost of any transfer from the manufacturing arm to the retailing arm includes the return that could have been made on a sale to an outsider.[169]

ATTORNEY: Let's examine some specific cases.

EXPERT: Yes.

ATTORNEY: In the cable television industry, the Federal Communications Commission recently found that cable operators have vertically integrated by acquiring "more and more interests in cable programming services and networks."[170] The FCC also reported that these vertically integrated cable operators now hold equity interests in thirteen of the top twenty basic cable networks and in six of the eight national

[167] Bork, *Antitrust Paradox*, 228.

[168] Sam Peltzman, "Issues in Vertical Integration Policy," in Weston and Peltzman, *Public Policy toward Mergers*, 171–72.

[169] Bork, *Antitrust Paradox*, 228.

[170] In re Competition, Rate Deregulation and the Commission's Policies Relating to the Provision of Cable Television Service, MM Docket No. 89–600 (July 31, 1990), 46.

pay cable networks.[171] And, significantly, it concluded that "the record shows that vertically integrated cable operators often have the ability to deny alternative multichannel media providers access to their vertically owned programming services,"[172] including charging access prices to nonintegrated rivals that are 36 percent to 78 percent higher than prices charged their own affiliates.[173] Similarly, in the airline industry, the General Accounting Office has reported that "airline-owned Computerized Reservation Systems (or CRSs) earn profits exceeding those that could reasonably be expected to be earned in a competitive market"; that "[t]hese high profits are earned through high booking fees and incremental revenues, which transfer profits from airlines that do not own CRSs to those that do"; and that "[t]his transfer artificially raises the costs of carriers not owning CRSs, making it more difficult for them to

[171] Ibid., 60.
[172] Ibid.
[173] Ibid., 60, tab. 11, app. G. Similarly, observing that "a few large vertically integrated firms control large segments of the domestic cable market," the House Committee on Energy and Commerce has reported that access to cable programming by potential cable competitors "has been limited and, in some cases, denied completely"; that fledgling new rivals attempting to compete are burdened with "severely discriminatory terms and conditions relative to those accorded cable operators," including program access prices in some cases as much as 460 percent higher than those charged the established companies' own affiliates; and that competitive growth in the industry "has been impeded, in part, by the unreasonable refusal of some [vertically integrated] video program vendors to deal with" these nonintegrated potential competitors. U.S. Congress, House, H. Rept. 682, *Cable Television Consumer Protection and Competition Act of 1989*, 101st Cong., 2d sess., 1990, 36, 40, 42, 44. For additional evidence, see U.S. Congress, Senate, Committee on Commerce, Science, and Transportation, Subcommittee on Communications, *Hearings on the Cable Television Consumer Protection Act of 1989*, 101st Cong., 2d sess., 1990, 274–87, 409–17.

compete in markets against a CRS vendor."[174] The GAO also reported that the eight major airlines together account for 90 percent of all gates leased at the nation's sixty-six largest airports, and that they sublease the gates needed by smaller carriers at rates three to eighteen times higher than the rates charged the major carriers by the airports.[175] Similar instances of integrated firms vertically squeezing their nonintegrated rivals have been documented in the oil industry,[176] the steel industry,[177] the cigarette in-

[174] U.S. Congress, House, *Hearings on the Adequacy of Competition in the Airline Industry*, 101st Cong., 1st sess., 1990, 292. See also U.S. General Accounting Office, *Airline Competition: Impact of Computerized Reservation Systems*, GAO/RCED-86-74 (May 1986). The GAO added that "[r]estrictive provisions in contracts between CRS vendors and travel agents regarding, for example, minimum use, make it virtually impossible for new airlines to start their own CRSs" (p. 17).

[175] U.S. General Accounting Office, *Airline Competition: Industry Operating and Marketing Practices Limit Market Entry*, GAO/RCED-90-147 (Aug. 1990), 42, 74.

[176] In oil, the vertically integrated majors have used their vertical pricing power to discipline, or to eliminate, nonintegrated independents, particularly low-priced discount operators at the retail stage. Recently, for example, Nevada gasoline dealers "uncovered what they claim is a blueprint Atlantic Richfield Co. used to raise its market share in the Las Vegas region to 42% from 5.5% between 1982 and 1987. To compete with the independents, the blueprint allegedly concluded that Arco needed to eliminate credit card business and push more gasoline through its own stations. To that end, Arco would systematically jack up the rent it charged existing dealers, which could cause 700 to 800 of them to quit. Many of those would be replaced by company-run facilities. There would be a period of lower profits, but a 'lasting period of quite acceptable profitability could ensue,' the plan concludes." Allanna Sullivan, "Small Gasoline Dealers Say Big Oil Is Pushing Them Out of Business," *Wall Street Journal*, Oct. 15, 1990, A-12. More generally, see Walter Adams and James W. Brock, "Deregulation or Divestiture: The Case of Petroleum Pipelines," *Wake Forest Law Review* 19 (1983): 705, and the documentation and sources cited therein; and U.S. Congress, Senate, *Petroleum Industry Competition Act of 1976*, 94th Cong., 2d sess., 1976, S. Rept. 1005, esp. 19–59.

[177] See Walter Adams, "Vertical Power, Dual Distribution, and the Squeeze: A Case Study in Steel," *Antitrust Bulletin*, May/June 1964, 493–508.

dustry,[178] and the telephone industry when it was controlled by the vertically integrated Bell monopoly.[179] Now, from your perspective as an economic scientist, doesn't such evidence suggest the capacity of vertically integrated firms to implement vertical price squeezes in order to forestall or to eliminate competition by nonintegrated rivals?

EXPERT: Regardless of what the bookkeeper writes down, the real cost is always the opportunity cost foregone. Nor would there be any point to a firm's subsidizing its retail level by transfers at artificially low prices.[180]

ATTORNEY: Why is that?

EXPERT: It would sacrifice profits at the manufacturing level, while the self-deception as to true costs would lead the retailing subsidiary to operate at an uneconomical rate.[181]

ATTORNEY: Suppose a vertically integrated firm elects to refuse to supply a necessary input to its nonintegrated rivals? Are you aware, for example, that this was an important reason for a U.S. district court rul-

---

[178] See American Tobacco Co. et al. v. United States, 328 U.S. 781 (1946), in which the Court found that the major cigarette producers squeezed independent "10-cent brands" from the market, in part by buying up the cheaper grades of leaf tobacco used by the independents, thereby raising the cost of this input and squeezing the independents' profit margins.

[179] In the case of interface equipment required by nonintegrated equipment producers to obtain access to the telephone system, for example, vertically integrated AT & T, "by controlling who could obtain [these devices], when, and at what cost, . . . was in a position to control the entry of potential competitors into the market." United States v. American Tel. & Tel. Co., 524 F. Supp. 1336, 1351 (D.D.C. 1981). The court also found that in the matter of long distance service, AT & T "attempted to deny competitors meaningful access to local distribution facilities by pricing access thereto discriminatorily . . ." (p. 1355).

[180] Bork, *Antitrust Paradox*, 228.

[181] Ibid.

ing blocking Mobil Oil's 1982 effort to acquire Marathon Oil,[182] and that the same problem led another U.S. district court to order the vertical divestiture of theaters by the nation's largest motion picture producers?[183]

EXPERT: Such a practice would be irrational.[184]

ATTORNEY: Why?

EXPERT: Because goods and services have market values outside the firm, and these opportunity costs must not be ignored.[185]

ATTORNEY: Are you familiar with what is referred to as the foreclosure effect of vertical mergers and vertical integration?

EXPERT: Yes. The argument is that manufacturer M acquires retailing firm R, forces its products on R, and thus forecloses other manufacturers from distributing through R.[186]

ATTORNEY: Now, isn't it a fact that in the motion picture industry, the Supreme Court found that by acquiring theaters, the major motion picture producers were able to control the industry, in part by foreclos-

---

[182] See Marathon Oil v. Mobil Corp., Trade Reg. Rep. 74,801 (Dec. 14, 1981), in which the tribunal found that Mobil Oil's attempted acquisition of Marathon would remove Marathon as an important supplier of refined gasoline to independent, nonintegrated gasoline retailers. On appeal, the appellate court found that "[b]ased on Mobil's past practice of selling gasoline only through Mobil stations, it seems unlikely that Mobil would continue to service the independents in times of shortage." Marathon Oil Co. v. Mobil Corp., 669 F.2d 378, 383 (6th Cir. 1981).

[183] United States v. Paramount Pictures et al., 85 F. Supp. 881 (S.D.N.Y. 1949). Generally, see Walter Adams and James W. Brock, "Vertical Integration, Monopoly Power, and Antitrust Policy: A Case Study of Video Entertainment," Wayne Law Review 36 (1989): 51, 55–63.

[184] McGee, Industrial Organization, 279.

[185] Ibid.

[186] Bork, "Vertical Integration," 146.

ing independent producers' access to key first-run theaters and in part by foreclosing independent theaters' access to the majors' movie productions?[187] Similarly, in the petroleum industry, hasn't the Federal Trade Commission recently documented the integrated majors' vertical capacity to control price-competitive independents by limiting their access to gasoline supplies?[188] And, again in the cable television field, hasn't the Federal Communications Commission found that vertically integrated cable firms have the ability to deny or unfairly place conditions on a program producer's access to local cable outlets?[189] As an economic scientist, don't you think such empirical evidence rather strongly suggests that vertical foreclosure can, in fact, lessen competition?

EXPERT: It is a theoretical impossibility.[190]

---

[187] United States v. Paramount Pictures et al., 334 U.S. 131 (1948). Similarly, vertical integration by the network television triopoly during the 1950s and 1960s effectively foreclosed independent producers of television programs from access to the broadcast television field. See Adams and Brock, "Vertical Integration, Monopoly Power, and Antitrust Policy," and the documentation and sources cited therein.

[188] "The most serious difficulty in entry or expansion faced by private brand independents may be the reluctance of the largest majors to sell wholesale gasoline to them ... When and where such wholesale gasoline supplies are available to such marketers, their lower costs and aggressive price-oriented marketing tend to encourage them to sell at low prices and to gain volume at the expense of the larger majors. Numerous company documents indicate that the largest eight majors each adopted a corporate policy of not selling gasoline to independent marketers." *Mergers in the Petroleum Industry: Report of the Federal Trade Commission* (Sept. 1982), 266.

[189] In re Competition, Rate Deregulation and the Commission's Policies Relating to the Provision of Cable Television Service, MM Docket No. 89–600 (July 31, 1990), 46, 70.

[190] Bork, "Vertical Integration," 146.

ATTORNEY: How can you say that? Aren't you engaging in what Lord Acton once called the "worst use of theory" —namely, "to make men insensible to fact"?[191]

EXPERT: Not at all. If the retail level of the market was in equilibrium before the vertical acquisition, then the existing pattern of distribution among retail outlets was optimal. If the vertically integrating firm were, say, to refuse to stock the products of its manufacturing rivals, it would change the distribution of brands in a way not desired by customers, thereby lowering the value of all retail outlets, including its own.[192]

ATTORNEY: All right, then. Let us turn to a third anticompetitive consequence of vertical integration. Isn't it true that a trend toward vertical integration in an industry raises barriers to new competition by concentrating control over existing trade channels in the hands of a few vertically integrated firms, by thinning the markets that formerly operated between these stages, and by effectively requiring that a new entrant enter the industry at multiple levels, rather than at a single stage?

EXPERT: The argument is illogical.[193]

ATTORNEY: Why is that?

EXPERT: To suppose that the need to enter an industry at two or more levels, rather than one, will deter entry when higher-than-competitive profits will re-

---

[191] Leo Rogin, *The Meaning and Validity of Economic Theory* (New York: Harper & Brothers, 1956), 309.

[192] Peltzman, "Issues in Vertical Integration Policy," 169.

[193] McGee, *Industrial Organization*, 279; Bork, *Antitrust Paradox*, 237.

ward entry relies on an unsubstantiated theory of artificial barriers to entry.[194]

ATTORNEY: But isn't it true that in the 1982 Mobil-Marathon merger case, for example, Mobil Oil's own internal documents concluded that new competitive entry into the field was "prohibitively expensive"?[195]

EXPERT: No such barriers exist in the economic world.[196] If greater than competitive profits are to be made in an industry, entry should occur whether the entrant has to come in on both levels at once or not.[197]

ATTORNEY: Why is that?

EXPERT: For the simple reason that there is no theory of imperfections in the capital market suggesting that suppliers of capital will avoid fields of higher return in order to seek fields of lower return.[198]

ATTORNEY: Your answer is interesting, given the fact that in your earlier testimony, you stated that vertical integration was a response to imperfections of the market. Would you please summarize for me your scientific view of vertical mergers and vertical integration?

EXPERT: There should be no concern about vertical integration by acquisition, growth, or contract.[199] On

[194] Bork, *Antitrust Paradox*, 241.

[195] The appellate court found that the "petroleum industry is characterized by high barriers to entry because of capital requirements" and that it was "unlikely that a new vertically integrated oil company would enter the market to take Marathon's place as . . . a supplier for independent dealers . . . . Mobil's own documents show that new entry is 'prohibitively expensive.' " Marathon Oil Co. v. Mobil Corp., 669 F.2d 378, 381 (6th Cir. 1981).

[196] Bork, *Antitrust Paradox*, 241.

[197] Bork, "Vertical Integration," 148.

[198] Ibid.

[199] Ibid., 149.

the contrary, vertical mergers should be encouraged.[200]

ATTORNEY: You must know that your position is at total variance with the views of your Chicago colleague, George Stigler. You must certainly recall Stigler's seminal article in which he argued that vertical integration may not be a problem per se, but that it "loses its innocence if there is an appreciable degree of market control at even one stage of the production process. It becomes a possible weapon for the exclusion of new rivals by increasing the capital requirements for entry into the combined integrated production processes, or it becomes a possible vehicle of price discrimination. In these cases," said Stigler, "new vertical mergers are not desirable." He recommended, therefore, that "where a firm has one fifth or more of an industry's output, its acquisition of more than five to ten percent of the output capacity of industries to which it sells or from which it buys in appreciable quantities shall be presumed to violate the antimerger law."[201]

EXPERT: That was Stigler's view some thirty years ago—long before he won the Nobel prize. He wouldn't embrace that position today.

JUDGE: This dialogue is edifying and at times fascinating. But it's been a long day, and I find myself drifting back to the days when I mediated snow removal priorities as a city official in Chicago. Unless there is an objection, let's stand in recess until ten o'clock tomorrow morning.

[200] Yale Brozen, *Concentration, Mergers, and Public Policy* (New York: Macmillan, 1982), 403.
[201] Stigler, "Mergers and Preventive Antitrust Policy," 183.

The Testimony on Conglomerate Mergers and Conglomerate Integration

JUDGE: Forecasting is fraught with error, but I'll go out on a limb and predict that you have some more questions for our expert.

ATTORNEY: That's correct, Your Honor.

JUDGE: Very well, then, please proceed.

ATTORNEY: Thank you, Your Honor. [*To the witness*] Are you familiar with the terms "conglomerate merger" and "conglomerate integration"?

EXPERT: Yes. A conglomerate merger is a merger between firms that are neither direct competitors nor in a buyer/seller relationship with each other within the same industry. Thus, a conglomerate merger would be any merger that is not horizontal or vertical. Conglomerate integration refers to a firm that operates in two or more unrelated markets and industries.

ATTORNEY: Would you provide an example of a conglomerate merger?

EXPERT: An example would be the purchase of a New York garment manufacturer by a California wine producer. The merger of the garment manufacturer and the wine producer is conglomerate because the firms do not sell in the same market and do not stand in a relation of supplier and customer.

ATTORNEY: Since the production operations of firms engaged in a conglomerate merger are, by definition, not related in any technological fashion, what is your scientific explanation for conglomerate mergers and conglomerate integration?

EXPERT: Conglomerates contribute valuable efficiencies.[202]

ATTORNEY: Even though the operations involved are technologically unrelated?

EXPERT: The conglomerate firm is capitalism's creative response to the limits of the capital market in its relation to the firm.[203]

ATTORNEY: Do you mean to say that the capital market, whose central function in a market system is to allocate investment funds among alternative projects and industries, is defective in some sense?

EXPERT: The capital market is a less than efficacious surveillance and correction mechanism.

ATTORNEY: But isn't it a fact that ITT, the premier conglomerator of the 1960s, has in recent years divested itself of approximately a hundred acquired operations, including oil and gas operations, Canadian timberlands, Continental Baking Company, and soda-bottling facilities?[204] Doesn't this suggest, as *Fortune* has pointed out, that ITT could acquire companies in diverse fields but was incapable of managing them effectively?[205] Given ITT's experience,

---

[202] Bork, *Antitrust Paradox*, 248.

[203] Williamson, *Markets and Hierarchies*, 159.

[204] Christopher Power, "How Cleaning House May Help ITT Clean Up," *Business Week*, Mar. 23, 1987, 64.

[205] Geoffrey Colvin, "The De-Geneening of ITT," *Fortune*, Jan. 11, 1982, 34.

how can you contend that conglomerates are superior to the outside capital market?

EXPERT: Because the capital market's external relation to the firm places it at a serious information disadvantage. It can make only nonmarginal adjustments. And it suffers nontrivial costs in correcting corporate behavior.[206]

ATTORNEY: But isn't it a fact that another leading conglomerate of the 1960s, Gulf & Western, turned itself into what has been called "a conceptually messy agglutination" of conglomerate operations, and that it, too, in recent years has shed some sixty businesses, ranging from sugar and zinc production, to cigar manufacturing and racetracks?[207] Given such empirical evidence, how can you claim that conglomerate administrative control over the allocation of investment funds is superior to control by the capital markets?

EXPERT: Because the conglomerate corporate organization has superior properties in three respects. First, it is an internal rather than external control mechanism, with the constitutional authority and expertise to make detailed evaluations of the performance of each of its operating parts. Second, it can make fine-tuning as well as discrete adjustments. Finally, the costs of intervention by the conglomerate's central offices are relatively low.[208]

ATTORNEY: Forgive me for dragging real world experience into this, but isn't it also a fact that General

---

[206] Williamson, *Markets and Hierarchies*, 158.

[207] Stewart Toy, "Splitting Up: The Other Side of Merger Mania," *Business Week*, July 1, 1985; and Laura Landro, "Reversing Course," *Wall Street Journal*, June 10, 1985, 1.

[208] Williamson, *Markets and Hierarchies*, 158–59.

Mills is now struggling to undo a loss-ridden conglomerate acquisition spree into such diverse fields as chemicals, luggage, two-person submarines, Play-Doh, Izod sportswear, and Monet jewelry, and that in recent years it has divested itself of some twenty-six businesses?[209] Yet it is your opinion that the market is an inefficient means for allocating a society's investment funds, as compared with allocation performed between divisions subsumed within the administrative control of a conglomerate organization?

EXPERT: If decisionmakers could be quickly and costlessly apprised of a wide range of alternatives and choose intelligently among them, there would be no reason to supplant the capital market with corporate conglomeration. But where complex events have to be evaluated, conglomerates have the information-processing capacities to reach decisions quickly, efficiently, and correctly.[210]

ATTORNEY: But hasn't *Forbes* magazine reported that the Big Oil firms, flush with cash in the 1970s, "handled the money badly, overpaying for fashionable diversification and overdosing on overhead," and that as a result, they dissipated their stockholders' funds in what *Forbes* characterizes as "overpriced and badly conceived diversification"?[211] Yet your theory concludes that organizational control displaces mar-

---

[209] Steve Weiner and Janis Bultman, "Calling Betty Crocker," *Forbes*, Aug. 8, 1988, 88; Alex Beam and Judith H. Dobrzynski, "General Mills: Toys Just Aren't Us," *Business Week*, Sept. 16, 1985, 106; Steven Prokesch, "New General Mills Is 'Lean and Mean,'" *New York Times*, Jan. 5, 1987, 19.

[210] Williamson, *Markets and Hierarchies*, 161–62.

[211] Toni Mack, "It's Time to Take Risks," *Forbes*, Oct. 6, 1986, 126.

ket allocation of capital because administrative control is better able to organize these complexities.

EXPERT: In an economy where allocation of investment funds by the capital market incurs nontrivial transaction costs, the internal allocation of resources to higher yield uses is what most commends the conglomerate firm. In these circumstances, the conglomerate assumes miniature capital market responsibilities of an energizing kind.[212]

ATTORNEY: [*Persisting*] But in steel, to take another example, if Armco Steel's conglomerate acquisition of insurance companies has generated a half-billion dollars in losses to date, if National Steel's diversification into pharmaceuticals and five-and-dime retailing (Ben Franklin stóres) has foundered, and if U.S. Steel has divested itself of chemical operations that languished under the firm's tutelage, how can you conclude that conglomerate mergers "energize" the allocation of society's financial capital?

EXPERT: Because the conglomerate's general office is supported by an elite staff that has the capacity to best evaluate divisional performance. Its improved information base enables it to assign rewards and penalties to divisions on a more discriminating basis and to allocate resources within the firm from less productive to more productive uses.[213]

ATTORNEY: So despite the empirical evidence, your scientific opinion is that when compared with the market form of organization, the conglomerate is a more efficient evaluator of alternative investment proj-

[212] Williamson, *Markets and Hierarchies*, 259–60.
[213] Williamson, *Economic Institutions* 284.

ects, and a more effective allocator of society's capital funds?

EXPERT: The conglomerate is best understood as a logical means for organizing complex economic affairs.[214]

ATTORNEY: In his recent study, Professor Michael Porter found the performance record of conglomerate acquisitions to be miserable, with an average failure
rate of 74 percent, as measured by divestiture of acquired operations.[215] And on the basis of the evidence amassed in their monumental study of mergers and acquisitions, Professors Ravenscraft and
Scherer conclude that "the internal capital market
theory of merger motives is subject to some serious
limitations."[216] Yet it is your scientific opinion that
conglomerate mergers rectify what you consider to
be the deficiencies of the outside capital market?

EXPERT: The benefits conglomerate acquisitions confer
include revitalizing sluggish companies, improving
managerial efficiency, and facilitating more effective
financial control systems.[217] Conglomerate mergers
are perhaps the most important means by which major chunks of industrial resources are moved from
the hands of less efficient managers to those of more
efficient managers.[218]

[214] Ibid., 288.
[215] Michael Porter, "From Competitive Advantage to Corporate Strategy," *Harvard Business Review* 65 (1987): 45.
[216] David J. Ravenscraft & F. M. Scherer, *Mergers, Sell-offs, and Economic Efficiency* (Washington, D.C.: Brookings Institution, 1987), 214. See
also Adams and Brock, *Dangerous Pursuits*, 96–99.
[217] Bork, *Antitrust Paradox*, 249.
[218] Prepared statement of William F. Baxter, in U.S. Congress, Senate,
Mergers and Economic Concentration: Hearings before the Subcommittee

ATTORNEY: Your points are well taken in theory, but they remind me of the anti-Enlightenment philosopher Johann Fichte, who insisted that so long as his conclusions were deduced rigidly and correctly, he saw no reason to inquire whether they were true in reality. Now I'd like to examine some anticompetitive consequences of conglomerate mergers.

EXPERT: Basic economic analysis confirms that conglomerate mergers pose no threat to competition.[219]

ATTORNEY: How do you reach that conclusion?

EXPERT: Like vertical mergers, conglomerate mergers don't combine rivals; therefore, they don't create or increase the ability to restrict output by increasing market share. Conglomerates do not threaten competition.[220]

JUDGE: Again, I must remind the witness that the Supreme Court has in the past blocked some conglomerate mergers, on the grounds that they threatened to substantially lessen competition or to tend to create a monopoly, in violation of section 7 of the Clayton Act. Surely, the witness is aware of the high court's decision in the Consolidated Foods case of 1965 and the Procter & Gamble case of 1967.[221]

EXPERT: With all due respect, Your Honor, I must insist that in these cases the Supreme Court cooked up a variety of esoteric and totally baseless theories about the harm caused by conglomerate mergers.[222]

---

on *Antitrust and Monopoly of the Committee on the Judiciary*, 96th Cong., 1st sess., 1979, pt. 2, 28.

[219] Bork, *Antitrust Paradox*, 246.

[220] Ibid., 248.

[221] FTC v. Consolidated Foods Corp., 380 U.S. 592 (1965); FTC v. Procter & Gamble Co., 386 U.S. 568 (1967).

[222] Robert E. Taylor, "A Talk with Antitrust Chief William Baxter," *Wall Street Journal*, Mar. 4, 1982, 22.

ATTORNEY: [*Resuming the examination*] Are you familiar with the phenomenon referred to as cross-subsidization, or the "deep pocket"?

EXPERT: The cross-subsidization criticism argues that various types of predatory behavior can occur in the large conglomerate firm because unprofitable activities can be subsidized by profitable ones. "Deep pocket" arguments are also directed at the ability of large firms to engage in heavy advertising that smaller firms cannot afford.[223]

ATTORNEY: You dismiss this concern?

EXPERT: The argument lacks plausibility in terms of general economic theory.[224]

ATTORNEY: Let's examine a specific example, the beer industry. Now isn't it a fact that a very large tobacco conglomerate, Philip Morris, acquired Miller Beer in the early 1970s; that it poured massive amounts into advertising its newly acquired Miller Beer subsidiary, absorbing sizable financial losses in the process; that this triggered a rapid horizontal combination movement, as other beer brewers merged in an attempt to match Miller's advertising; and that the result has been to dramatically raise the market share of the four largest firms in the industry, from 47 percent in 1972, to 86 percent by 1988, with the share of the two largest firms, Busch and Miller, now standing at nearly 70 percent?[225] How, then, can you

[223] J. Fred Weston, *Mergers and Economic Efficiency*, vol. 2, *Industrial Concentration, Mergers and Growth* (Washington, D.C.: U.S. Dept. of Commerce, June 1981), 56.

[224] Ibid.

[225] U.S. Congress, Senate, *Mergers and Industrial Concentration: Hearings before the Subcommittee on Antitrust and Monopoly of the Committee on the Judiciary*, 95th Cong., 2d sess., 1978, 84–124; Willard F. Mueller,

argue that the anticompetitive aspects of such cross-subsidization are implausible?

EXPERT: Because if a firm finds some activities are unprofitable, it is better to dispose of them than to subsidize them. If demand response is not sufficiently high in relation to cost outlays, the activity is unprofitable and will not be pursued by a company acting rationally.[226]

ATTORNEY: Moving to a second area, are you familiar with a practice referred to as reciprocal dealing?

EXPERT: Reciprocity is the practice under which one company makes its purchase decisions depend on its volume of sales to another company, rather than on competitive and product quality.[227] It is generally defined as the practice of favoring those suppliers who also buy from you.[228]

ATTORNEY: Doesn't such reciprocal dealing lessen competition, especially when a large conglomerate firm, with diversified activities, utilizes the practice across the many markets in which it operates?

EXPERT: Your claim has no foundation in economic theory.

ATTORNEY: Why is that?

"Conglomerates: A 'Nonindustry,' " in Walter Adams, ed., *The Structure of American Industry*, 8th ed. (New York: Macmillan, 1990), 330–33; John M. Connor et al., *The Food Manufacturing Industries: Structures, Strategies, Performance, and Policies* (Lexington, Mass.: Lexington Books, 1985), 244–59; "Anheuser's Plan to Flatten Miller's Head," *Business Week*, Apr. 21, 1980, 171; and Tim Metz, "Recession-Resistant Brewing Industry Is Seen Becoming Highly Concentrated and Profitable," *Wall Street Journal*, Aug. 28, 1979, 37.

[226] Weston, *Mergers and Economic Efficiency*, 56.

[227] Ibid., 57.

[228] Prepared statement of Jesse W. Markham, in Senate, *Mergers and Economic Concentration*, pt. 1, 428.

EXPERT: Because where a firm has market power, it can use that power directly. Reciprocal buying arrangements cannot enhance market power.[229]

ATTORNEY: But isn't it true, for example, that following General Dynamics' acquisition of an industrial gas producer, Liquid Carbonics, Judge Cannella found a prime motive for the merger to have been stated by the firm's management to be "to aid the Liquid Carbonic sales picture via General Dynamics' reciprocity leverage"; that as a result of the merger, Liquid Carbonics would, according to the firm's management, "have at its disposal the entire purchasing power of General Dynamics' other divisions for reciprocal buying purposes"; and that General Dynamics ceased buying from suppliers who refused to procure their industrial gases from its Liquid Carbonics subsidiary?[230]

EXPERT: I have heard tenuous conjectures concerning reciprocal dealing.[231] It is nothing more than the standard leverage fallacy in another context.[232]

ATTORNEY: But isn't it also the case that General Tire—a conglomerate with operations in tire manufacturing, airlines, tennis ball production, and radio and television stations—was found by the Federal Communications Commission to have conducted an

[229] George J. Benston, *Conglomerate Mergers: Causes, Consequences and Remedies* (Washington, D.C.: American Enterprise Institute, 1980), 27.

[230] United States v. General Dynamics Corp., 258 F. Supp. 36, 42–47 (1966).

[231] Prepared statement of Richard A. Posner, in Senate, *Mergers and Economic Concentration*, pt. 2, 10.

[232] Bork, *Antitrust Paradox*, 258.

intensive program of reciprocal dealing, whereby firms were induced to advertise on General's radio stations as a condition of doing business with any of General's other divisions?[233] Given this empirical evidence, on what do you base your conclusion that conglomerate reciprocity is a fallacy?

EXPERT: It contradicts economic logic. For a large conglomerate, the required recordkeeping to practice such reciprocity would be unduly burdensome and complicated.[234]

ATTORNEY: But is it not a fact that General Motors, for example, used its automobile shipments with railroads as a lever for reciprocal dealing, by conveying that railroads purchasing their locomotives from GM's locomotive division would be rewarded with shipment orders to transport GM autos?[235] Don't these empirical examples contradict your theory that reciprocity is benign?

EXPERT: Not at all. If the practice leads to efficiency, there is little reason to stop it. If it leads to ineffi-

---

[233] Willard F. Mueller, "Conglomerates: A 'Nonindustry,' " in Walter Adams, ed., *The Structure of American Industry*, 7th ed. (New York: Macmillan, 1986), 275.

[234] Prepared statement of Jesse Markham, in Senate, *Mergers and Economic Concentration*, pt. 1, 428–29.

[235] For example, the president of the Baltimore & Ohio Railroad was contacted by General Motors officials regarding a GM offer to locate one of its warehouses near B & O tracks, in return for the railroad's agreement to purchase locomotives from GM. According to analyst B. C. Snell, B & O's president replied to GM by letter to the effect: "Here is your Christmas present . . . we will purchase 300 diesel locomotives . . . we now expect to receive a New Year's gift from you . . . locate your warehouse near our tracks." U.S. Congress, Senate, *The Industrial Reorganization Act: Hearings before the Subcommittee on Antitrust and Monopoly of the Committee on the Judiciary*, 93d Cong., 2d sess., 1974, pt. 4A, 38–40, 39.

ciency, there is little reason to suppose that it would be widely adopted or last for long since it would reduce the firm's overall profits.[236]

ATTORNEY: But isn't it true that after reporting that reciprocal "trade relations between the giant conglomerates tend to close a business circle," and that "as patterns of trade and trading partners emerge between particular groups of companies, entry by newcomers becomes more difficult," *Fortune* magazine warned that "the United States economy might end up completely dominated by conglomerates happily trading with each other in a new kind of cartel system"?[237] In the face of such evidence, is it your scientific opinion that reciprocal dealing has no anticompetitive consequences?

EXPERT: It is clear that reciprocity has absolutely no effect on competition whatsoever.[238]

ATTORNEY: I would like to turn now to the topic of competitive forebearance by conglomerates. You are familiar with the term?

EXPERT: Yes. The argument is as follows: If large conglomerate X sells widgets, gadgets, and gewgaws, and large conglomerate Y sells widgets, gewgaws, and gimcracks, X will not compete vigorously with Y in the widget market because this would be an open in-

[236] Prepared statement of James C. Miller III, Chairman, Federal Trade Commission, in U.S. Congress, Senate, *Oversight of Government Merger Enforcement Policy: Hearings before the Committee on the Judiciary*, 97th Cong., 1st sess., 1982, pt. 1, 91.

[237] *Fortune*, June 1965, 194.

[238] Testimony of William F. Baxter, in U.S. Congress, House, *Mergers and Acquisitions: Oversight Hearings before the Subcommittee on Monopolies and Commercial Law of the Committee on the Judiciary*, 97th Cong., 1st sess., 1983, 184.

vitation to Y to compete vigorously with X in the gewgaw market. Corporation Y will presumably adopt a similar policy of competitive forebearance.[239]

ATTORNEY: Suppose we examine something a little more substantial than gimcracks and gewgaws. During the 1920s, it seems Exxon's refining activities were becoming increasingly chemical in nature, and the firm began to contemplate entry into chemical markets. At the same time, a large German chemical concern, IG Farben, was making impressive technological breakthroughs in the production of synthetic gasoline from coal. The firms thus could have entered each other's fields and competed head to head. Instead, they struck a "marriage agreement," the essence of which was described by an Exxon official as providing that the "IG are going to stay out of the oil business proper and we are going to stay out of the chemical business insofar as that has no bearing on the oil business."[240]

EXPERT: Yes.

ATTORNEY: In fact, Sir Alfred Mond, organizer of the giant British chemical combine ICI Limited, long ago observed that the "old idea of the heads of great businesses meeting each other with scowls and shaking each other's fists in each other's faces and . . . trying to destroy each other's business may be very good on the films, but it does not accord with any given

[239] Senate, *Mergers and Economic Concentration*, 429.

[240] See George W. Stocking and Myron W. Watkins, *Cartels in Action* (New York: Twentieth Century Fund, 1946), 91–93, 491–95; and U.S. Congress, Senate, *Economic and Political Aspects of International Cartels*, report prepared by Corwin D. Edwards for the Subcommittee on War Mobilization of the Committee on Military Affairs, 78th Cong., 2d sess., 1944, Committee Print, 27.

facts."[241] As officials of du Pont, another sizable firm, expressed it, "It is not good business sense to attempt an expansion in certain directions if such an act is bound to result in a boomerang of retaliation,"[242] because in the long run, "the boot was just as likely to be on one leg as on the other."[243] Now doesn't this suggest that competitive forbearance among large conglomerate firms might, in fact, occur?

EXPERT: For conglomerate firms operating in many markets to avoid competition would be difficult.[244] Balancing the gains from forbearance in one market against the losses in another would be an impossibly complicated task.[245]

ATTORNEY: As you know, aggregate concentration refers to the share of economic activity collectively accounted for by the largest firms in the economy, regardless of the particular markets and industries in which they operate.

EXPERT: Yes.

ATTORNEY: It measures the extent to which the general economy is concentrated in the hands of the very largest firms. Now, is it not true that as the nation's

[241] Quoted in Stocking and Watkins, *Cartels in Action*, 429.

[242] Quoted in U.S. Congress, Senate, *Economic Concentration: Hearings before the Subcommittee on Antitrust and Monopoly of the Committee on the Judiciary*, pt. 8A, *Economic Report on Corporate Mergers: Staff Report of the Federal Trade Commission*, 91st Cong., 1st sess., 1969, 462.

[243] Ibid. As a du Pont official articulated it to the German chemical firm of Farben, "in any field of manufacture where it appears that the situation makes it desirable to enter each others' market," economic self-interest dictates "we get together and see if we cannot negotiate an arrangement for cooperation." Quoted in Senate, *Economic and Political Aspects of International Cartels*, 8.

[244] Weston, *Mergers and Economic Efficiency*, 57.

[245] Benston, *Conglomerate Mergers*, 31.

largest firms diversify by engaging in large conglomerate acquisitions, the degree of aggregate concentration in the economy is raised and that, as a result,
fewer organizations come to control a larger aggregate share of the economy?[246]

EXPERT: I'm never quite sure what people mean when
they talk about concentrations of power.[247]

ATTORNEY: I mean the degree to which a small number
of very large firms collectively control a large share
of the nation's economic decisionmaking.

EXPERT: It is not particularly disturbing to me.[248]

ATTORNEY: But as an advocate for the market system,
would you not be disturbed by an escalating degree
of aggregate concentration? Would it not indicate
that proportionately less economic activity was gov-
erned by the market, and that proportionately more
of it was being centrally administered within conglomerate organizations—that is, outside the market?

[246] For evidence that the wave of large conglomerate mergers and acquisitions during the 1960s and 1970s significantly raised aggregate concentration in the American economy, see U.S. Congress, House, The Celler-Kefauver Act: The First 27 Years, study prepared by Willard F. Mueller for the
Subcommittee on Monopolies and Commercial Law of the Committee on
the Judiciary, 96th Cong., 1st sess., 1980, 82–83.

[247] Interview with Assistant Attorney General William F. Baxter, U.S.
News & World Report, Aug. 3, 1981, 51.

For in-depth analyses, see Walter Adams and James W. Brock, The Bigness Complex (New York: Pantheon Books, 1987); and Wallace C. Peter-
son, ed., Market Power and the Economy (London: Kluwer Publishers,
1988), esp. Douglas Greer, "The Concentration of Economic Power," 53–
82. For conglomerates in particular, see Mueller, "Conglomerates: A 'Nonindustry,' " in Walter Adams, ed., The Structure of American Industry; and
Corwin D. Edwards, "Conglomerate Bigness as a Source of Power," in National Bureau of Economic Research, Business Concentration and Price
Policy (National Bureau of Economic Research, 1955), 331–52.

[248] "Big Shift in Antitrust Policy," Dun's Review, Aug. 1981, 38.

EXPERT: There is nothing written in the sky that says that the world would not be a perfectly satisfactory place if there were only a hundred companies.[249]

ATTORNEY: But the shrinking role for the market . . .

EXPERT: A formidable antitrust challenge in the conglomerate area would seriously affect market mechanisms necessary for the transfer of assets to their most productive uses.[250]

ATTORNEY: But if the essence of the huge, multiproduct, multimarket conglomerate firm is to combine a vast array of unrelated products and operations under a single, centralized administrative management, then would it not be accurate to say that the ultimate conglomerate is the centrally planned Soviet state?[251]

EXPERT: Obviously, such a parallel would be theoretically invalid.

ATTORNEY: Why is that?

EXPERT: Because the conglomerate firm operates in the private sector, but the Soviet state does not.

The Testimony on Corporate Deal Mania Generally

ATTORNEY: If we may, I would like to turn now in a more general way to the American corporate deal mania of the 1980s.

---

[249] Ibid.

[250] Prepared statement of James C. Miller III, in Senate, *Oversight of Government Merger Enforcement Policy*, 92.

[251] It is the zeal for rationality and efficiency, says Hayek, that explains the flirtation of some economists with centralized socialist planning. Hayek sees this as an important consequence of the abuse of reason in the social sciences. See Hayek, *Counter-Revolution of Science*.

EXPERT: Yes.

ATTORNEY: As you know, corporate deals of all types—mergers, acquisitions, hostile raids, and leveraged buyouts—erupted during the decade. The number of corporate deals leaped from 1,565 in 1980 to 3,487 by 1988; their combined annual value jumped from $33 billion in 1980 to $227 billion in 1988; and the number of megadeals valued at $1 billion or more skyrocketed, from three in 1980 to forty-two by 1988. All told, more than a trillion dollars were expended on these corporate deals during the decade of the 1980s.[252]

EXPERT: Yes.

ATTORNEY: And if you would examine Exhibit 2, which my assistant has just placed on the easel, you will see that to finance this unprecedented penchant for corporate dealmaking, corporate debt—fueled by junk bonds—also jumped during the period, from

EXHIBIT 2. JUNK BONDS AND TOTAL CORPORATE DEBT OF U.S. COMPANIES, 1980–1987 (BILLIONS OF DOLLARS)

Year	Total Bonds and Notes Issued	Junk Bonds Issued
1980	42.5	0.9
1981	37.3	1.2
1982	44.7	1.5
1983	50.1	3.6
1984	68.7	7.4
1985	89.7	8.0
1986	177.5	24.3
1987	191.3	26.1

Source: Economic Report of the President, 1989, 415; Barry Wigmore, "The Decline in Quality of Junk Bond Issues, 1980–1988" (unpublished manuscript, 1988).

[252] Adams and Brock, Dangerous Pursuits, 11–12.

$43 billion of corporate debt issues in 1980, to $191 billion by 1987—a growth rate of 350 percent over the period.[253] As one result, the share of corporate pretax profits consumed by interest expenses on corporate debt doubled over the decade, reaching a level of 44 percent by 1988.[254]

EXPERT: Yes.

ATTORNEY: Now, as an economic scientist, how would you assess this unprecedented phenomenon?

EXPERT: My approach is to assume that the people who are spending their money to bring about those mergers and whose motivation can only be to make more money are those most likely to be right in judging which mergers will enhance productivity.

ATTORNEY: Why do you make that assumption?

EXPERT: Because the only way they can make more money is to make the assets they have bought produce more productively in their hands than they were producing in the hands of those from whom they were bought. They are putting their money where their mouths are. They are making wagers.[255]

ATTORNEY: Would you elaborate on your assumption?

EXPERT: Certainly. The market for corporate control is an arena in which alternative management teams compete for the rights to manage corporate resources.

---

[253] Statement of Walter Adams and James W. Brock, U.S. Congress, House, *Leveraged Buyouts and Bankruptcy: Hearings Before the Subcommittee on Economic and Commercial Law*, 101st Cong., 2d sess., 1991.

[254] Ibid., exhibit 10.

[255] Testimony of William F. Baxter, in U.S. Congress, Senate *Productivity in the American Economy, 1982: Hearings before the Subcommittee on Employment and Productivity of the Committee on Labor and Human Resources*, 97th Cong., 2d sess., 1982, 495.

ATTORNEY: But aren't you ignoring the capacity of insiders in these deals—incumbent managements and raiders alike—to feather their own nests at the expense of stockholders and the firms' economic performance? In Matsushita's recent acquisition of MCA, for example, MCA's president received a bonus of $21 million for arranging the deal, and an increase in his salary from $900,000 to $8.6 million per year.[256] A recent deal with Scandanavian Airlines enabled Frank Lorenzo to unload his shares in Continental Airlines—a debt-burdened money loser, since he purchased it as a vehicle for further acquisitions—only months before the firm declared bankruptcy, and at a price twice that available in the stockmarket to other stockholders.[257] The management of Metromedia took that company private, paying stockholders $724 million for a firm that turned out to be worth at least six times that amount.[258] And is it not the case, as John Kenneth Galbraith has observed and as a parade of convicted felons attests, that the paths of financial dealmaking lead regularly, if not to the grave, at least to the minimum security slammer?[259]

EXPERT: Be that as it may, these corporate restructurings play an important role in generating organiza-

---

[256] Richard Turner and Randall Smith, "MCA's Sheinberg to Receive $21 Million as Bonus in 5-Year Matsushita Contract," *Wall Street Journal*, Dec. 3, 1990, A6.

[257] Floyd Norris, "A Good Deal for Lorenzo," *New York Times*, Aug. 10, 1990, C8.

[258] "Where Are the Shareholders' Yachts? But John Kluge Pockets Billions from Metromedia LBO," *Barron's*, Aug. 18, 1987, 100. For a discussion of additional examples, see Adams and Brock, *Dangerous Pursuits*, 44–56, 74–79, 107–13.

[259] John K. Galbraith, "From Stupidity to Cupidity," *New York Review of Books*, Nov. 24, 1988, 12.

tional change, motivating the efficient allocation of resources, and protecting shareholders when the corporation's internal controls and board-level controls are slow, are clumsy, or break down entirely.[260]

ATTORNEY: Aren't you also ignoring the possibility that astronomical legal and investment banking fees—perhaps as high as half a billion dollars in the case of the RJR-Nabisco buyout alone—play a major role in fueling the dealmaking flames? According to *Forbes* magazine, the mint that Wall Street makes from takeovers "may do more to explain current merger mania than all the blather about synergy and diversification."[261] Again, quoting from *Forbes*, "Why are people willing to pay $21 billion for a cracker-and-tobacco company [RJR-Nabisco]? Wrong question. Better ask: Who on Wall Street profits from the madness?"[262]

EXPERT: No market is frictionless. The fees to which you refer, and the banking and legal services provided, lubricate the market for corporate control, and facilitate its functioning.

ATTORNEY: And the extremely heavy corporate debt loads built up in the process?

---

[260] Testimony of Professor Michael C. Jensen, in U.S. Congress, House, *Impact of Mergers and Acquisitions: Hearings before the Subcommittee on Telecommunications and Finance of the Committee on Energy and Commerce*, 100th Cong., 1st sess., 1987.

[261] Richard Phalon, "Fuel for the Flames," *Forbes*, Nov. 18, 1985, 122. For one in-depth analysis of how a major investment banking firm "restructured" a corporation by drawing off more than $100 million in advising fees, loading the firm down with debt, selling off some of its key income-generating operations, and then bailing out just as the economic downturn struck the financially weakened enterprise, see George Anders, "Morgan Stanley Found a Gold Mine of Fees by Buying Burlington," *Wall Street Journal*, Dec. 14, 1990, A1.

[262] Allan Sloan, "When the Music Stops," *Forbes*, Nov. 14, 1988, 44.

EXPERT: They, too, are beneficial, because they encourage cuts in programs and sales of operations that are more valuable outside the firm, and they force a rethinking of the organization's strategy and structure.[263]

ATTORNEY: Are you aware that in recent years, however, an alarming number of these highly leveraged corporate deals have begun to collapse, with the firms either already in bankruptcy or on the verge of being forced into bankruptcy?

EXPERT: Yes.

ATTORNEY: Are you aware, for example, that this list of failed, or failing, firms now includes the Campeau Corporation (including its Bloomingdale's, Burdines, Lazarus, and Jordan Marsh stores);[264] the retailers Bonwit Teller, B. Altman,[265] Garfinckel's,[266] Ames Department Stores,[267] and Macy's;[268] the Southland (Seven-11 stores)[269] and Circle K[270] convenience stores; Supermarkets General;[271] Interco, producer of

[263] Testimony of Michael C. Jensen, in House, *Impact of Mergers and Acquisitions*, 135.

[264] Carol J. Loomis, "The Biggest Looniest Deal Ever," *Fortune*, June 18, 1990, 48.

[265] Mark Potts, "The High Price of Buying Retail," *Washington Post*, national weekly edition, Oct. 16–22, 1989, 23.

[266] Edmund L. Andrews, "First Altman's, Now Garfinckel's," *New York Times*, June 28, 1990, C1.

[267] Joseph Pereira and Jeffrey A. Trachtenberg, "Ames Seeks Protection under Chapter 11 after Retailer's Talks with Lenders Stall," *Wall Street Journal*, Apr. 27, 1990, A3.

[268] N. R. Kleinfield, "Stemming the Losses," *New York Times*, Mar. 18, 1990, sec. 3, p. 5.

[269] Kevin Helliker, "Southland Files for Protection under Chapter 11," *Wall Street Journal*, Oct. 25, 1990, A3.

[270] Sonia L. Nazario, "Circle K Squares Off with Its Creditors," *Wall Street Journal*, May 17, 1990, A7.

[271] Floyd Norris, "An Ailing Buyout Tries a Buyback," *New York Times*, Nov. 26, 1990, C4.

Lane-Broyhill furniture, and Florsheim and Converse shoes;[272] Continental,[273] Braniff,[274] and TWA[275] airlines; Heileman Brewing (the nation's third-largest brewer)[276] and Vintner's International Company (Paul Masson and Taylor wines);[277] Unisys (the merged Sperry and Burroughs computer firms);[278] the textile firms West Point-Pepperell[279] and J. P. Stevens;[280] the Jim Walter Corporation[281] and National Gypsum;[282] the Fruehauf[283] and Leaseway[284] trucking operations; Revco Drug Stores;[285] the publishers

[272] Brian Bremner, "Interco: Another Day Older and $1.4 Billion in Debt," *Business Week*, Jan. 22, 1990, 58; George Anders and Francine Schwadel, "Wall Streeters Helped Interco Defeat Raiders—But at a Heavy Price," *Wall Street Journal*, July 11, 1990, A1.

[273] Bridget O'Brian, "Debt-Burdened Continental Air, Citing Rising Fuel Costs, Files under Chapter 11," *Wall Street Journal*, Dec. 4, 1990, A3.

[274] Charles Crumpley, "Braniff Blueprint: Small Investment, Big Gains," *Kansas City Times*, Oct. 27, 1989, A1.

[275] Agis Salpukas, "Icahn on TWA Woe," *New York Times*, Feb. 10, 1990, 17.

[276] Marj Charlier, "Brewer Heileman Files under Chapter 11," *Wall Street Journal*, Jan. 25, 1991, B6.

[277] Lawrence M. Fisher, "A Troubled Winery Where Debt is Aging," *New York Times*, May 12, 1990, 17.

[278] Paul Carroll, "Unisys Struggles in Dire Computer-Industry Straits," *Wall Street Journal*, Oct. 4, 1990, A8.

[279] Rick Christie and Robert Johnson, "West Point–Pepperell Twists in the Wind," *Wall Street Journal*, Feb. 21, 1990, A6.

[280] George Anders, "JPS Textile to Restructure Its Debt Loan," *Wall Street Journal*, Dec. 24, 1990, 11.

[281] David B. Hilder and Randall Smith, "Kohlberg Kravis Sails into Rough Waters with Hillsborough Unit Chapter 11 Filing," *Wall Street Journal*, Dec. 29, 1989, C1.

[282] Karen Blumenthal, "National Gypsum and Parent Seek Chapter 11 Status," *Wall Street Journal*, Oct. 30, 1990, A9.

[283] Joseph B. White, "Fruehauf, Overloaded with Buy-Out Debt, Will Be Dismembered," *Wall Street Journal*, Mar. 29, 1989, A1.

[284] Zachary Schiller, "Leaseway May Set a Standard for Ailing LBOs," *Business Week*, Nov. 27, 1989, 81.

[285] Gregory Stricharchuk, "Revco's Leveraged Buy-Out Comes Apart," *Wall Street Journal*, June 14, 1988, 6.

Ingersoll[286] and Harcourt Brace Jovanovich;[287] the
First Executive Insurance Company;[288] and the very
kingpin promotor of junk bonds and corporate deals,
the Drexel Burnham investment house?[289] As an economic scientist, surely you do not consider such empirical evidence to be irrelevant?

EXPERT: Critics of the activity of recent years have con-
tended that many specific mergers have been fail-
ures, from which they conclude that mergers in general are counterproductive transactions. This kind of
anecdotal approach is not an acceptable scientific basis for forming public policy, however.[290]

ATTORNEY: Are you aware that the quality of the debt
issued by these presumably more efficient firms is
being downgraded by independent bond-rating agen-
cies at a record rate?[291]

EXPERT: Yes.

ATTORNEY: Are you aware that these presumably more
efficient corporate organizations are defaulting on
their debts at record high rates?[292] If I could invite

---

[286] Patrick M. Reilly, "Ralph Ingersoll Finds Newspapers Are Fun, Junk
Bonds Are Not," *Wall Street Journal*, Mar. 26, 1990, A1.

[287] Leslie Wayne, "Can Harcourt Brace Survive Its Debt?" *New York
Times*, Apr. 15, 1990, sec. 3, p. 1.

[288] For a revealing analysis, see Benjamin Stein, "Sunk by Junk," *Barron's*, April 1, 1991, 8.

[289] Michael Siconolfi et al., "Wall Street Era Ends as Drexel Burnham Decides to Liquidate," *Wall Street Journal*, Feb. 14, 1990, A1.

[290] Interview with Douglas H. Ginsburg, Assistant Attorney General, Antitrust Division, Department of Justice, *Antitrust Law Journal* 55 (1986):
255, 256.

[291] "Record Pace for Corporate Downgradings," *New York Times*, Oct.
12, 1990, C12; Roger Lowenstein, "Junk Gets Junkier," *Wall Street Journal*,
Nov. 3, 1989, C1.

[292] Richard D. Hylton, "Corporate Bond Defaults Up Sharply in '89,"
New York Times, Nov. 11, 1990, 25; Ralph E. Winter and Thomas F.
O'Boyle, "Bankruptcy-Law Filings by Firms Spurt," *Wall Street Journal*,

your attention to Exhibit 3, which my assistant has just placed on the easel, you'll see that the value of assets of insolvent public companies in 1990 was fully 550 percent higher than four years earlier.

EXPERT: Yes, I know.

ATTORNEY: Isn't it becoming more and more apparent, therefore, that the deal mania of the 1980s created excessively high debt loads, which firms seem increasingly incapable of carrying?[293] Moreover, didn't

EXHIBIT 3. ASSETS OF ALL U.S. PUBLIC COMPANIES
ENTERING BANKRUPTCY PROCEEDINGS, 1986–1990
(BILLIONS OF DOLLARS)

Year	Total Assets
1986	12.7
1987	40.7
1988	43.5
1989	66.6
1990	82.7

Source: Wall Street Journal, Fortune.

Apr. 6, 1990, A2; Matthew Winkler, "Junk Bond Market Is Seen Showing 38% Default Rate," Wall Street Journal, Jan. 25, 1990, C20; Floyd Norris, "As Defaults Keep Rising, a Market Dies," New York Times, Sept. 9, 1990, sec. 3, p. 1; Lindley H. Clark and Alfred L. Malabre, "Takeover Trend Helps Push Corporate Debt and Defaults Upward," Wall Street Journal, Mar. 15, 1988, A1.

[293] See, for example, Christopher Farrell and Leah Nathans, "The Bills Are Coming Due," Business Week, Sept. 11, 1989, 84; Fred Bleakley, "Many Firms Find Debt They Piled On in 1980s Is a Cruel Taskmaster," Wall Street Journal, Oct. 9, 1990, A1; Larry Light, Jon Friedman, and John Meehan, "All That Leverage Comes Home to Roost," Business Week, Sept. 10, 1990, 76; Jason Zweig and David Stix, "Tick, Tick, Tick," Forbes, Aug. 6, 1990, 78; Gary Hector, "Junk's Bad Times Are Just Starting," Fortune, June 4, 1990, 81; Larry Light and Leah Nathans, "The Junk-Bond Time Bombs Could Go Off," Business Week, Apr. 9, 1990, 68; Sarah Bartlett, "Cracks in House That Debt Built," New York Times, Aug. 17, 1989, 25; David Vise, "The Chickens May Be Coming Home to Declare Bankruptcy," Washington Post, national weekly edition, Jan. 22–28, 1990, 20;

all the adverse developments we have just discussed emerge during relatively robust economic conditions, prior to the 1990 weakness of the American economy? Aren't you denying the evidence of facts that you deem not to be in accordance with the nature of things.[294]

EXPERT: Not at all. Some deals, of course, will fail. But when the corporate dealmakers make mistakes, they pay heavy penalties, and the market works there too.[295]

ATTORNEY: Would you explain how?

EXPERT: If a corporate deal works out, then everyone benefits. If it fails, it will be undone, and again there will be no economic harm. For example, as President Reagan's Council of Economic Advisers has forcefully reminded us, we musn't forget that one distinguishing characteristic of the current merger experience is the prevalence of divestiture transactions, reflecting a trend away from the failed conglomerate mergers of the 1960s and 1970s, and intended to better focus the firms' operations.[296]

ATTORNEY: But aside from your admission that mergers are not automatically efficiency enhancing, aren't

Matthew Winkler, David Hilder, and James White, "Mounting Losses Are Watershed Event for Era of Junk Bonds," Wall Street Journal, Sept. 18, 1989, A1; David Vise and Steven Mufson, "The Buyouts That Are Going Bust," Washington Post, national weekly edition, Aug. 28–Sept. 3, 1989, 8; "Defaults of the Future," Grant's Interest Rate Observer, Oct. 27, 1989, 2–10.

[294] This was a criticism leveled against the nineteenth-century economist Jean Baptiste Say, who gained fame as the author of Say's law. See Rogin, The Meaning and Validity of Economic Theory, 231.

[295] Testimony of William F. Baxter, in U.S. Congress, Senate, Hearings on Productivity in the American Economy, 97th Cong., 2d sess., 1982, 495.

[296] Economic Report of the President, 1985, 195.

you failing to consider the economist's concept of opportunity cost—the fundamental economic principle that there is no such thing as a free lunch, that the choice of doing A unavoidably entails the cost of not doing B?

EXPERT: Merger activity in general is a very, very important feature of our capital markets, by which assets are continuously moved into the hands of those who can employ them efficiently. Interfering with corporate deals would be an error of very substantial magnitude.[297] Our primary national concern must be for U.S. industry's ability to restructure in order to meet the competitive challenge of its efficient foreign rivals.[298]

ATTORNEY: But even if we ignore the expanding empirical record of failed or failing corporate deals, is it not the case that when viewed in an opportunity cost context, the managerial energies and the approximately one trillion dollars devoted to the paper entrepreurialism of the 1980s could, instead, have been directly invested in constructing new plants, installing new equipment, building new products, and undertaking new research and development initiatives?

EXPERT: Once again, you commit a fundamental economic fallacy.

ATTORNEY: How is that?

---

[297] William F. Baxter, Assistant Attorney General, Antitrust Division, Department of Justice, quoted in Bob Gatty, "Antitrust Goal: Economic Rationality," *Nation's Business*, Oct. 1981, 59.

[298] Charles Rule, Assistant Attorney General, Antitrust Division, Department of Justice, quoted in Fred Barnes, "For Bush Aides, Confusion Is Spelled A-N-T-I-T-R-U-S-T," *Business Month*, Jan. 1989, 19.

EXPERT: The reason is obvious. If an acquiring firm had more profitable capital investment or research and development opportunities available, it would find it profitable to take advantage of them, rather than acquiring other firms. Since it chooses not to invest in such socially preferable alternatives, they obviously do not exist.[299]

ATTORNEY: Well, as Freud said, theory is good but it doesn't prevent things from existing. Exhibit 4, which is now on the easel, depicts corporate America's spending on mergers and acquisitions, research and development, and net new nonresidential investment during the 1980s. I would like to invite

EXHIBIT 4. EXPENDITURES OF ALL U.S. CORPORATIONS ON MERGERS, RESEARCH AND DEVELOPMENT, AND NET NEW INVESTMENT, 1980–1986 (BILLIONS OF DOLLARS)

	Total Expenditures		
Year	Mergers and Acquisitions	R & D	Net New Nonresidential Investment
1980	33.0	30.9	88.9
1981	67.3	35.9	98.6
1982	60.4	40.1	65.5
1983	52.6	43.5	45.8
1984	126.0	49.1	91.1
1985	145.4	52.6	101.5
1986	204.4	55.7	81.0

Source: Walter Adams and James W. Brock, *Dangerous Pursuits: Mergers and Acquisitions in the Age of Wall Street* (New York: Pantheon Books, 1989), 123.

[299] Benston, *Conglomerate Mergers*, 52.

your attention especially to the entries for 1986, the bottom row in the table.

EXPERT: What about them?

ATTORNEY: Those entries reveal that in 1986, corporate America spent more on deals than it did on research and development and net new investment combined.

EXPERT: Yes. I am capable of performing simple addition.

ATTORNEY: Fine. I would also invite your attention to the contrast between Japanese and American corporate priorities. In 1988, total Japanese capital investment exceeded that of American firms by an estimated $250 billion—despite the fact that the American economy is some 40 percent larger than that of Japan.[300] On a per capita basis, Japanese firms have been outinvesting American firms by a two-to-one margin.[301] And over the 1985–1988 period, Japanese firms increased their combined expenditures for factories, equipment, and research and development by an estimated 150 percent, compared to an increase of only 23 percent by American firms over the same period.[302]

EXPERT: Yes.

ATTORNEY: [Continuing] But American firms spent approximately $204 billion on mergers and acquisitions in 1986, while Japanese firms are estimated to

[300] David Sanger, "Japan Keeps Up the Big Spending to Maintain Its Industrial Might," New York Times, Apr. 11, 1990, 1.
[301] Carla Rapoport, "Japan's Capital Spending Spree," Fortune, Apr. 9, 1990, 91.
[302] Ibid.

have spent only $3 billion on corporate deals in the same year.[303]

EXPERT: That may have been true in the past, but the Japanese have recently begun to make some major cross-national acquisitions, such as Sony's purchase of Columbia Pictures and CBS Records, Bridgestone's purchase of Firestone Tires, and Matsushita's purchase of MCA.

ATTORNEY: I also invite your attention to the recent concerns voiced by the National Science Foundation concerning the adverse impact of corporate deals on the nation's research and development efforts. While conceding that it is too early fully to assess the long-term effects, the National Science Foundation's study of twenty-four companies found that sixteen companies that had undergone mergers and acquisitions showed a 4.7 percent drop in research and development spending in 1986 and 1987 and eight companies that had undertaken leveraged buyouts or other restructurings showed an even steeper 12 percent drop.[304]

EXPERT: Yes.

ATTORNEY: Now, I ask you, from an economic point of view, aren't investments in plant and equipment and research and development the kinds of investments that ultimately determine a nation's competitive performance in the long run? And if so, is it not the case that investing in corporate deals instead of making these kinds of real investments unavoidably ex-

[303] The Economist, Mar. 21, 1987, 94.
[304] Fortune, Mar. 13, 1989, 98.

acts an enormous opportunity cost in terms of diminished national competitiveness? And, further, if these spending patterns reflect our national priorities, then should we really be surprised that we are losing markets to foreign producers, who, after all, have been investing in building better products and producing them in better facilities?

EXPERT: When you see a merger or an acquisition of assets occur, what it involves is one party saying, I think I can take those assets that another party now has and make them more valuable in my hands.[305]

ATTORNEY: Yes, I understand that. But you just spoke of divestitures as a way for firms to rectify their misguided conglomerate acquisition and diversification forays of the 1960s and 1970s. My question to you is, don't these divestitures, and the failed conglomerate acquisitions that gave rise to them, merely return us back to where we were in the 1950s, while our global competitors are poised to move ahead into the twenty-first century? And isn't this really the measure of the opportunity cost to the nation of playing the game of corporate deal mania on the scale and magnitude we witnessed during the 1980s?

EXPERT: This amounts to nothing more than a recognition of the obvious point that businesspeople sometimes err, and it is quite irrelevant to antitrust policy.[306]

---

[305] Testimony of Charles Rule, Assistant Attorney General, Antitrust Division, Department of Justice, in U.S. Congress, Senate, *Authorization Legislation and Oversight of the U.S. Department of Justice: Hearings before the Committee on the Judiciary*, 100th Cong., 1st sess., 1988, 21.

[306] Interview with Douglas H. Ginsburg, *Antitrust Law Journal* 55 (1986): 256.

ATTORNEY: Let me try to make this more concrete. F. Ross Johnson rose to the top of Standard Brands, and then, in 1981, he merged Standard with Nabisco in a $2 billion deal. According to your theory, was that deal designed to enhance the economic efficiency of the combined firm, Nabisco Brands?

EXPERT: Yes.

ATTORNEY: Mr. Johnson subsequently rose to the top of Nabisco Brands, and then, in 1985, merged Nabisco Brands with tobacco giant R. J. Reynolds—again, according to your economic theory, in order to enhance the economic efficiency of the combined firms, RJR-Nabisco?

EXPERT: That's right.

ATTORNEY: But then in 1988, in one of the most notorious corporate battles of the 1980s, F. Ross Johnson proposed to buy out RJR-Nabisco, to take it private, and to break it apart—again, according to your theory, in order to enhance economic efficiency. Viewed from the initial merger in 1981 to the proposed bust-up in 1988, would you say that this represents a productive use of society's scarce economic resources?[307]

EXPERT: I repeat: The dealmakers are the individuals who are out there in the merger market betting their own money.[308]

ATTORNEY: You keep saying the dealmakers bet their own money. But if we put their failure record to the side, and even if we ignore the fact that innocent

---

[307] Adams and Brock, *Dangerous Pursuits*, 16–17, 49–50.

[308] U.S. Congress, Senate, *Hearings on Authorization Legislation and Oversight of the U.S. Department of Justice*, 100th Cong., 1st sess., 1988, pt. 2, 20.

people far removed from the deals have lost savings, pensions,[309] and jobs because of these financial shenanigans, isn't it still the case that, when companies invest in deals instead of new products, factories, equipment, and research and development, *all* of society pays the price in terms of less innovation, lower productivity, loss of markets to foreign producers, with concomitant losses of jobs, production, and technical expertise in the United States, and an erosion of our nation's industrial base? For example, does the name Akio Morita ring a bell?

EXPERT: Yes, he is the chairman of the board and chief executive officer of Japan's highly successful Sony Corporation.

ATTORNEY: Mr. Morita insists that the key to national competitiveness—to which you repeatedly refer—is increased investment, strengthened research and development, and work force development. And he adds that it typically takes years to develop a new manufacturing technology, to apply it to a product, and to turn the product into a profitable business.[310] Now, is it not the case that as a short-run game played for short-run paper profits, corporate deal mania fundamentally conflicts with the longer-term perspective that Morita describes, which the empirical record shows that he and his Sony firm have implemented in the global marketplace with considerable success?

[309] Frederic Rose and David Wessell, "Junk Bond Woes Put Retirement Benefits in Danger for Many," *Wall Street Journal*, Feb. 12, 1990, A1.

[310] Akio Morita, "Something Basic Is Wrong in America," *New York Times*, Oct. 1, 1989, sec. 3, p. 2.

EXPERT: Short-term profits are better than long-term profits.[311]

ATTORNEY: I'm afraid I don't follow you.

EXPERT: Short-term profits are better because they don't have to be discounted over a long time.[312]

JUDGE: I think that's enough erudition for one day. We stand adjourned until tomorrow morning at nine o'clock.

[311] Interview with Assistant Attorney General William F. Baxter, *U.S. News & World Report*, Aug. 3, 1981, 51.
[312] Ibid.

Day 4 – The Impact of Economic Power Is Discussed; Public Policy Interests in Economic Liberty and Democratic Process Yield a Conundrum

JUDGE: I should like to admonish the attorney that this voir dire has taken more time than I had anticipated. We still have a lengthy trial before us, and we must avoid the temptation to string out these proceedings.

ATTORNEY: I understand, Your Honor, and I promise to finish examining the witness by lunch this morning.

JUDGE: I cannot help but recall the old *Alcoa* case, which was launched in 1937 and wasn't resolved until 1950. At the time I was a young attorney in the Justice Department, and heard a story making the rounds in the antitrust division. One of the attorneys on the case asked for an adjournment till the next day, saying that he had been to the telephone and been advised that a son had been born to him. The judge said, "My memory is good and I remember that you made the same plea some time ago in the course of this trial." The attorney replied, "That was three years ago, Your Honor, and this plea is as valid as the one I made at that time." "Very well," said the judge, "we shall decree an adjournment on condition that there will be no adjournments in this case because of the birth of grandchildren."

ATTORNEY: I shall try to expedite matters as much as is reasonably possible.

JUDGE: Very well, then, proceed.

ATTORNEY: Thank you, Your Honor. [*To the witness*] Finally, I'd like to explore your views of government policy in a more general sense. What, in your opinion, constitutes the major source of market power in a free enterprise economy?

EXPERT: The only important source of long-lasting monopoly is the government.[313]

ATTORNEY: Why is that?

EXPERT: Because the government wields powers of coercion not available to private parties, and it frequently deploys these to throttle competition.[314]

ATTORNEY: Would you provide some illustrative examples?

EXPERT: The cartelization by government of transportation, utility, communication, and agricultural industries; legislated protection through licensing of professions and trades; protection from foreign competition through tariffs and other import restrictions—these restraints dwarf any private monopolization that may occur.[315]

ATTORNEY: You include government restraints on foreign competition in your list?

[313] Harold Demsetz, "The Trust behind Antitrust," in Eleanor M. Fox and James T. Halverson, eds., *Industrial Concentration and the Market System* (Chicago: American Bar Association, 1979), 51. See also Daniel T. Oliver, Chairman, Federal Trade Commission, Luncheon Address, reprinted in *Antitrust Law Journal* 55 (1985): 349.

[314] Demsetz, "Trust behind Antitrust," 51.

[315] Ibid.

EXPERT: The federal government's most substantial restraints on competition arise from the multitude of
barriers to international trade that have been erected
over the years, and that continue to be erected, by
statute and through administrative proceedings.[316]

ATTORNEY: And you consider such government protectionism harmful?

EXPERT: When I say that governments hurt their citizens by restraining international trade, I don't mean
to suggest that all citizens are hurt. Inefficient domestic producers certainly benefit, as do their employees, when imports are restricted. But the people
as a whole—the consumers—suffer.[317] The American
consumer today pays involuntary subsidies on a
massive scale to industries that have won special
protection.[318]

ATTORNEY: And what is your opinion of government
bailouts of large firms, such as Chrysler and Lockheed, when they confront imminent bankruptcy?

EXPERT: Our private enterprise system is a profit and
loss system. The fundamental principle of this system is that private industry assumes risks and takes
the consequences of its actions. If government is to
guarantee against losses, it is entitled to determine
what ventures enterprises undertake. This would be
a step away from the free enterprise society and toward a collectivist society.[319] If government social-

---

[316] Oliver, Luncheon Address, 353.

[317] Ibid., 354.

[318] Daniel T. Oliver, Chairman, Federal Trade Commission, Address to
Fordham Corporate Law Institute, reprinted in *FTC Newsnotes*, Oct. 27,
1986.

[319] Letter submitted by Professor Milton Friedman, in U.S. Congress,
Senate, *Emergency Loan Guarantee Legislation: Hearings before the Com-*

izes the losses, it will inevitably end up socializing the profits.[320]

ATTORNEY: But is it not the case that in a representative democracy, the state is deliberately designed to be responsive to the citizenry and consequently the government doesn't act in a vacuum. In this political context, do you have an opinion as to how it is that government is perverted into an instrument for creating market power, and for obstructing competition?

EXPERT: The state interferes with competition because it is lobbied by the politically strong—that is, the relatively wealthy—who face an uncertain future at the hands of the market.[321]

ATTORNEY: Are you saying that economic power wields anticompetitive influence, with antisocial consequences, in the political arenas in which government policy is fashioned?

EXPERT: Together, the politically strong and our legislators devise measures to limit competition from those who are politically weaker.[322]

ATTORNEY: Yet throughout the course of this proceeding, you consistently and repeatedly have criticized antitrust when it is directed toward dissolving structurally concentrated monopoly and oligopoly or when it is employed to stop merger-induced trends toward greater concentrations of private market power.

mittee on Banking, Housing and Urban Affairs, 92d Cong., 1st sess., 1971, 1172.

[320] Milton Friedman, " 'No' to More Money for the IMF," Newsweek, Nov. 14, 1983, 96.

[321] Oliver, Luncheon Address, 350.

[322] Ibid. For a masterful exploration of this problem, see Morton Mintz and Jerry S. Cohen, Power, Inc. (New York: Viking Press, 1976).

EXPERT: The drive for intervention on any handy theory comes out of a frustrated socialist impulse whose intellectual apparatus is gibberish.[323]

ATTORNEY: But are you aware, that some of the most influential advocates of private enterprise have historically feared disproportionate private economic size and power, precisely because of its unique political capacity to manipulate government, and to generate the kinds of antisocial government practices that you claim to abhor? For example, since his image adorns your tie, I assume you are familiar with the writings of Adam Smith, the great eighteenth-century economic libertarian?

EXPERT: Of course.

ATTORNEY: Then may I invite your attention to Book 4, Chapter 8, of his treatise *The Wealth of Nations*, where Smith points out that "the cruellest of our revenue laws, I will venture to affirm, are mild and gentle, in comparison of some of those which the clamour of our merchants and manufacturers has extorted from the legislature, for the support of their own absurd and oppressive monopolies."[324]

EXPERT: Yes, I remember the passage.

ATTORNEY: Would it not be accurate to say that Adam Smith recognized the untoward impact of economic power on the political process and public policy, and that he viewed the mercantilist state of his day as a perfect example of the corruption of government by powerful private economic interests?

EXPERT: Yes.

[323] Robert H. Bork, "Are We Counting the Real Costs?" in Fox and Halverson, *Industrial Concentration and the Market System*, 271.
[324] Adam Smith, *The Wealth of Nations* (reprint, New York: Modern Library, 1937), 612.

ATTORNEY: Again, in *The Wealth of Nations*, criticizing the strangling web of monopolies and anticompetitive restraints imposed by the Crown, Adam Smith observed "how contrary such regulations are to the boasted liberty of the subject, of which we affect to be so very jealous; but which, in this case, is so plainly sacrificed to the futile interests of our merchants and manufacturers." He went on to point out that "it cannot be very difficult to determine who have been the contrivers of this whole mercantile system; not the consumers, we may believe, whose interest has been entirely neglected; but the producers, whose interest has been so carefully attended to; and among this latter class our merchants and manufacturers have been by far the principal architects."

EXPERT: I can assure you that I am quite familiar with the *Wealth of Nations*. I have boundless admiration for its author, and, as you have pointed out, I even wear an Adam Smith tie.

ATTORNEY: Now, continuing, are you familiar with the works of Friedrich von Hayek, a prominent economic libertarian of the twentieth century?

EXPERT: Yes.

ATTORNEY: Are you aware that after concluding that "the industrial protectionism and government-supported cartels of the conservative groups are not different from the proposals for a more far-reaching direction of economic life sponsored by the socialists," even Hayek conceded that to protect the democratic state from the depradations of private economic power, "[t]here may be valid arguments for so designing corporation law so as to impede the indefinite growth of individual corporations"?[325]

EXPERT: Yes.

ATTORNEY: Are you aware that in his libertarian manifesto, *The Road to Serfdom*, Hayek warned that capitalist organizers of monopolies constitute one of the two most serious threats to a free society (the other being organized labor), and that he feared "a state which allows such enormous aggregations of power to grow up cannot afford to let this power rest entirely in private control"?[326]

EXPERT: Although the discredited, anticonsumer antitrust policies of yesteryear may be in repose, they are not wholly forgotten.[327]

ATTORNEY: You are familiar with the writings of Professor Henry C. Simons?

EXPERT: Certainly. He was a distinguished member of the economics faculty at the University of Chicago for many years.

ATTORNEY: Then are you aware that in his classic treatise, *Economic Policy for A Free Society*, Professor Simons categorically stated that "the great enemy of democracy is monopoly, in all its forms";[328] that he concluded that "[e]ffectively organized functional groups"—including "gigantic corporations"—"possess tremendous power for exploiting the commu-

[325] Friedrich A. Hayek, *Individualism and Economic Order* (Chicago: University of Chicago Press, 1948), 107, 116.

[326] Friedrich A. Hayek, *The Road to Serfdom* (Chicago: University of Chicago Press, 1944), 194–95.

[327] Interview with Daniel Oliver, *Antitrust Law Journal* 56 (1981): 239, 244.

[328] Henry C. Simons, *Economic Policy for a Free Society* (Chicago: University of Chicago Press, 1948), 43.

nity at large and even for sabotaging the system";[329]
and that he warned that in "an economy of intricate
division of labor, every large organized group is in a
position at any time to disrupt or to stop the whole
flow of social income; and the system must soon
break down if groups persist in exercising that power
or if they must continuously be bribed to forgo its
disastrous exercise"?[330]

EXPERT: Yes.

ATTORNEY: Are you aware that Professor Simons insisted that there is "no reasonable excuse (the utili-
ties aside) for hundred-million-dollar corporations,
no matter what form their property may take," and
that even "if the much-advertised economies of gigantic financial combinations were real, sound policy would wisely sacrifice these economies to preservation of more economic freedom and equality"?[331]

EXPERT: Yes.

ATTORNEY: Are you aware that Professor Simons insisted that "no one may be trusted with much
power," including corporations, and that he wrote
that "[p]olitical insight reveals that concentration of
power is inherently dangerous and degrading; economic insight reveals that it is quite unneces-
sary"?[332] And are you aware that because he considered so serious the threat that powerful private
economic interests would capture the democratic
state that Simons—an avowed libertarian—categorically called for an "outright dismantling of our giant

[329] Ibid.
[330] Ibid., 122.
[331] Ibid., 52.
[332] Ibid., 241.

corporations" and for legislation that "must prohibit
... the acquisition by any private firm, or group of
firms, of substantial monopoly power, regardless of
how reasonably that power may appear to be exercised," including an outright "[l]imitation upon the
total amount of property which any single corporation
may own"?[333] How do you respond to Simons's fears
regarding the political dangers of private economic
power?

EXPERT: The answer, I believe, is that in earlier years
the field of economics that studies monopoly questions tended to be untheoretical, descriptive, insti-
tutional, and even metaphorical. The result was that
propositions were regularly advanced that contra-
dicted economic theory.[334]

ATTORNEY: Permit me to make this a bit more concrete. You criticize government restraints on foreign
competition and government bailouts of large failing
firms, and you admit that such counterproductive
government folly stems, at bottom, from political influence exercised by the economically powerful?

EXPERT: Political freedom is inextricably intertwined
with economic freedom. Constant kowtowing by
Congress to special interests renders the democratic
process rather less useful to those whose economic
interest is best served by vigorous competition.[335]

ATTORNEY: But if you permit such private size and aggregate concentration in the private sector, then how
does a free society prevent the coercive power of the

[333] Ibid., 58–59.
[334] Richard Posner, "The Chicago School of Antitrust Analysis," University of Pennsylvania Law Review 127 (1979): 925, 928–29.
[335] Oliver Luncheon Address, 349, 357.

state from being captured in the political arena? Isn't this the political-economic problem recognized by Adam Smith, Hayek, and Simons? For example, when corporations attain the size of a Chrysler or a Lockheed, does not experience demonstrate that as a matter of political reality, they become too large and too important to too many to be allowed to fail?

EXPERT: As I recall it, it was Lord Keynes who said, "Owe your banker a thousand pounds and you are at his mercy. Owe him one million and the position is reversed."

ATTORNEY: [Continuing] And when their performance deteriorates and they confront the painful corrective of foreign competition, does not experience demonstrate that huge firms, such as the Big Three in the automobile industry or the largest steel producers, do not meekly sacrifice themselves on the altar of private enterprise but, instead, mobilize their vast political resources—executives, employees, trade unions, suppliers, subcontractors, dealers, mayors and governors, senators and representatives, Republicans and Democrats—and successfully demand government protection?

EXPERT: When we turn to antitrust analysis we are not concerned with aggregate concentration or with absolute size.[336]

ATTORNEY: But if that is your position, isn't making government less responsive and hence less accountable to the citizenry the only remaining way to protect the state from encroachment by powerful private interests? And as Hayek and Simons feared,

[336] Interview with Douglas H. Ginsburg, 255, 259.

would that not represent an important step toward a despotic state?

EXPERT: Pronouncements about the need for antitrust policy to shake off the confining theorems of scientific economics are nothing new. From the outset, antitrust has suffered from the vapid notion that it somehow comprised social and political aspirations. The difficulty with this conjecture is that it is impossible to tell what anybody is talking about.[337]

ATTORNEY: Nevertheless, you wouldn't deny, would you, that the concentration of power, whether in private hands or in the hands of the state, carries with it the potential—indeed, the probability—of abuse? You wouldn't deny, would you, that the potential for abuse that flows from the concentration of power is inimical to the preservation of a free society? You wouldn't deny, would you, that a decentralized power structure is at the very root of America's political democracy and the American brand of free enterprise economics?[338]

EXPERT: I believe that the concentration of power in the hands of the state is far more dangerous than any private concentration of power.

ATTORNEY: That is a value judgment rather than a scientific conclusion, isn't it?

---

[337] Bork, "Are We Counting the Real Costs?" 270.

[338] See, for example, James Madison, *Notes of Debates in the Federal Convention of 1787* (New York: W. W. Norton & Co., 1987 ed.); Alexander Hamilton, James Madison, and John Jay, *The Federalist Papers* (New York: New American Library, 1961 ed.); Adams and Brock, *The Bigness Complex*, 87–103; David Millon, "The Sherman Act and the Balance of Power," *Southern California Law Review* 61 (1988): 1219; James May, "Antitrust in the Formative Era: Political and Economic Theory in Constitutional and Antitrust Analysis, 1880–1918," *Ohio State Law Journal* 50 (1989): 257.

EXPERT: Yes, if you want to put it that way.

ATTORNEY: In conclusion, let's see whether we can agree on two fundamental propositions. First, is it fair to say that the New Learning rests on a preference for liberty of contract and the associated ideal of competition free from government power, whereas traditional antitrust rests on a preference for eliminating gross inequalities in the marketplace and the associated ideal of competition free from private power? Is it fair to say that the New Learning proceeds from an unmitigated commitment to individual liberty, which is understood as antithetical to a commitment to equality, whereas the critics of the New Learning adhere to the view that a strong commitment to a balanced power structure is entirely consistent with a strong commitment to individual liberty?[339]

EXPERT: That is a fair way of stating the essence of the controversy.

JUDGE: I'm afraid this debate could go on interminably without reaching a conclusion. We all say we believe in liberty, but what is liberty to one person is tyranny to another. As Abraham Lincoln put it, "The shepherd drives the wolf from the sheep's throat, for which the sheep thanks the shepherd as a *liberator*, while the wolf denounces him for the same act as the destroyer of liberty. . . . Plainly the sheep and the wolf are not agreed upon a definition of the word liberty. . . ."[340]

---

[339] Rudolph J. Peritz, "A Counter-History of Antitrust Law," *Duke Law Journal*, 1990, 310.

[340] Abraham Lincoln, Address at a Sanitary Fair in Baltimore, Apr. 18,

ATTORNEY: Thank you, Your Honor. I have only one more question. [*Turning to the witness*] Would you agree that the wisdom of Frank Knight, the grand master of the old Chicago school, applies to the New Learning as it does to any economic theory? Would you agree that, as Knight insisted, the main injunctions of economics are essentially negative: not to go too fast, not to oversimplify, not to grasp at easy solutions for hard problems?[341] Would you agree with his admonition that in economic theory, as in cookery, prudence calls for enough and not too much, far enough and not too far, in any direction?[342]

EXPERT: As you say in the legal profession, I have to take it under advisement.

ATTORNEY: Your Honor, I have no further questions.

1864, reprinted in Roy P. Basler, ed., *Abraham Lincoln: His Speeches and Writings* (Cleveland and New York: World Publishing Co., 1946), 749.

[341] F. Knight, *On the History and Method of Economics* (Chicago: University of Chicago Press, 1956), 280.

[342] Ibid., 256.

INDEX